Data Quality Control—A New Research Technique

RAOUL NAROLL

Data Quality Control—
A New Research Technique

Prolegomena to a Cross-Cultural Study

of Culture Stress

The Free Press of Glencoe

Acknowledgments

This research was supported by Grants M-1930 and M-2453, National Institutes of Health, U.S. Public Health Service. I began preliminary work on the methodology involved here while a Fellow at the Center for Advanced Study in the Behavioral Sciences. For my training in library research methods, I am deeply indebted to Professors Brainerd Dyer and Truesdell S. Brown. Martin Reif served as research assistant, Norman Henderson as psychological consultant. David Hays, statistical consultant, gave invaluable help. Other colleagues were also generous with suggestions, advice, encouragement and criticism: Franz Alexander, Ralph Beals, Robert Carneiro, Carleton Coon, Gertrude E. Dole, Harold Driver, Fred Eggan, Joseph B. Ford, Helen Giedt, John P. Gillin, Walter Goldschmidt, Ralph Greenson, John Higham, John J. Honigmann, W. W. Howells, Herbert Kelman, Clyde Kluckhohn, Ruth Landes, Clement W. Meighan, Frada Naroll, Ruth Nicks, Marvin Opler, Philip Sapir, Nora Weckler, Elizabeth Q. White, and the men of the San Fernando Valley State College Chowder and Marching Society. Frances Wishard and Helen Azhderian of the Library of the University of Southern California gave cooperation far beyond the call of duty. Dale Baker, Sue Binder, Penny McFadden, and Frada Naroll worked on the manuscript. Vital administrative advice and help was given by Philip Sapir and Irving Simos of the National Institute of Health and by Warner Masters and William Lerz of the San Fernando Valley State College Foundation. Of course, I alone am responsible for errors and shortcomings. Thanks are due to the editors of *The American Journal of Obstetrics and Gynecology*, *The International Journal of Social Psychiatry*, and *The Symposia Studies Series* for permission to republish material first published by them.

San Fernando Valley State College
    Northridge, California
       September, 1960

Contents

Acknowledgments

CHAPTER 1

Theory of Data Quality Control

INTRODUCTION

This work is a study of the reliability of some ethnographic data of interest in culture stress research. While the problem of data reliability is a special concern in culture stress research, it is a general problem that concerns every social scientist. Surely every social scientist who works with oral or written reports needs to be concerned about their accuracy. The historian or political scientist who works with records, letters, memoirs, and chronicles; the ethnographer who works with native informants; the comparative ethnologist who works with the reports of ethnographers; the sociologist or social psychologist who works with case files; the economist who works with statistical reports—all need to be suspicious of the reliability of the reports from which they compile data. For more than a century the only systematic method of evaluating the reliability of reports has been the method of internal and external criticism developed by classical historians.* This monograph offers a new method—data quality control.

The classical methods of internal and external criticism have lately fallen out of fashion in anthropology, sociology, and social psychology—perhaps because they depend so much on the personal judgment of the investigator. Although classical source criticism sometimes leads to complete rejection of a purported source, it never results in objectively verifiable confirmation of the validity of a source. Indeed, the traditional methods of selection and criticism of sources have seemed so subjective that they have led historians like Croce and Beard to despair of the whole process. This monograph offers a way out of the dilemma through data quality control.

Data quality control deals not with individual reports but instead with groups of reports compiled by various authors under various conditions. It depends upon the assumption that some records are made under conditions of higher apparent trustworthiness than others. For example, some reports about primitive tribes are made by people who have stayed years among them, while other reports are made by people who have stayed with the natives only a day or two; some reports are made by people who know the native language intimately, and other reports are made by people who do not know it at all but must trust to interpreters. Another example: some reports about battles of the American Civil War were written on the day of the fight, and others from memory decades later; some reports were written by soldiers with no responsibility for the course of events—

---

* By *reliability* I mean here general trustworthiness; and by *reports* I mean here descriptions of human behavior in a form and structure supplied by the observer. I am not talking about mere *consistency of responses* to tests or other questionnaires, thus not about mere "reliability" in the sense the word is usually used by social psychologists.

and hence with no decisions to justify or mistakes to cover up—while other reports were written by the generals in charge with their reputations in mind.

Data quality control deals not merely with isolated facts but also—and much more important—with hypotheses about correlations. In much social science research the key question is not whether or not errors of any kind occur in the data, but, instead, whether or not the errors that occur tend to make spurious correlations. Systematic biases may tend to make spurious correlations, or they may tend to destroy the evidence that a correlation exists when in fact it does. Random errors almost always tend to reduce the size of observed correlations, and the probability that they instead produce a spurious correlation is easily established. Data quality control offers a way to control the effect upon correlations not only of bias in data reports but also of random error there.

An investigation that tests hypotheses about correlations specified in advance and that tests the reliability of the data through data quality control solves the problem of subjective bias of the investigator as it influences his selection of source material and his evaluation of its reliability; thus it solves the problem of historical research method that seemed insuperable to Beard, Croce, and so many other historians. The cross-cultural survey method of anthropology is a good example of the possibilities and problems of this kind of correlational research. The use of data quality control in cross-cultural surveys is demonstrated in this book.

Data quality control uses statistical reasoning somewhat like that in industrial production quality control. It systematically compares data from reports made under better conditions with those made under worse conditions to see if they differ seriously. This method can test for special bias in both qualitative (yes-or-no) and quantitative data. Furthermore, in quantitative data it can also test for the existence of random error resulting from poor reporting conditions.

For example, in this book a test shows that ethnographers who have stayed longer than a year with the natives they describe are more likely to report high rates of witchcraft attribution than those who have stayed a shorter time. Other tests suggest the possibility of similar tendencies in reports of suicide and homicide rates. But equally important, another test fails to show a like tendency in reports of drunken brawling: apparently a brief stay among natives is usually enough to find out reliably whether they are given to drunken brawling or not. Thus the presence of a reporting bias is shown for witchcraft attribution and suggested for homicide and suicide, and the absence of a serious reporting bias is suggested for drunken brawling. As another example, this book shows that among the tribes studied population estimates have a smaller variance than official population censuses—a finding that makes it seem unlikely that population estimates are any more subject to random error than official population censuses.

This book also shows how to deal with random error of another kind—chance variations in rate of occurrences among small populations. Thus it shows that (other considerations apart) a report of three suicides in 80 years among the 600-800 Toda people is not reliable evidence of a long-term rate under 10 per 2,000 per 50-year period, although a report of only one suicide in 80 years would have been reliable evidence (if otherwise satisfactory).

This book is not a manual, not a how-to-do-it textbook. Instead, it is a demonstration of the use of the method in a research problem where data reliability is a crucial question. The book then is not a blueprint; it is a working model. It shows how to control the reliability of data by actually controlling some. The data controlled come from a cross-cultural survey of 37 societies, mostly primitive tribes; they deal with the number of people, and frequency of drunken brawling, homicide, suicide and witchcraft attribution, determined largely from the Human Relations Area Files. The data are used to construct a tentative index of culture stress. The underlying theory of cultural stress is discussed, and the place of such an index in culture stress research is suggested. Thus, although this report is in no sense a test of culture stress theory or of the value of the tentative index of culture stress, it presents in data quality control a tool that could and should play an essential part in any future test of culture stress theory in general or of the tentative culture stress index in particular. The thesis of this report is that a valid cross-cultural survey, testing a theory of culture stress through the use of the tentative culture stress index here proposed, is not barred by the unreliability of data in existing ethnographic reports. Through the data quality control techniques here described and demonstrated, the social scientist can control biases and random errors in reports of population size and of rates of suicide, homicide, drunken brawling, and witchcraft attribution.

HISTORY OF THE DATA QUALITY CONTROL PROBLEM

The only approach to statistical data quality control in library research known to me has been in cross-cultural surveys of ethnological data. Here the combination of classical source criticism training and statistical orientation logically points toward statistical data quality control. However, even in cross-cultural surveys, the approach has been very slow. Indeed, any kind of source criticism in cross-cultural surveys has been surprisingly rare.

The need seems obvious enough. The tradition of source criticism in classical scholarship was already firmly established as the cornerstone of historical investigation when Tylor introduced the cross-cultural survey in 1889. Yet the only cross-cultural survey to assess the reliability of its sources formally and systematically is buried today in a rarely cited Viennese periodical, and its example has gone ignored for more than sixty years. In *Endokannibalismus,* the first cross-cultural survey to publish data as well as conclusions, Steinmetz [1] classified the data on each people in his sample in five grades of source reliability. He classed as Grade 1 data from a source "where the report comes from a recognizedly good observer who was in the position to make good observations after an acquaintance of some time with the people concerned and where furthermore the report is not in conflict with our other information or where the report comes unanimously from several observers without any contradictions"; as Grade 2 data from a "relatively good field worker under average conditions but not beyond doubt"; as Grade 3 data from any source, however respectable, that was disputed by some other observer; as Grade 4 data from a source of doubtful reliability in the absence of any specific challenge to the statement in question; and as Grade 5 data that for one reason or another seemed to him highly questionable.

While some of Steinmetz' students discussed the reliability of their sources in passing, none followed his example of systematically rating them. The English and American comparativists who developed the cross-cultural survey method largely lost sight of Steinmetz and his school until Köbben [2] reminded the world of their work, but no one—not even Köbben—seems to have paid attention to the *Endokannibalismus* paper. The only attention to data quality control given in English or American cross-cultural surveys has been that by Beatrice Whiting [3] and by John Whiting and Irvin Child.[4] In both these studies, the authors limited their attention to the evaluation of the reliability of inferences about traits studied made by the comparativists from mere hints or suggestions in the field reports. For example, an ethnographer who does not say whether or not sorcery is important may nevertheless describe it at some length. The comparativist must decide subjectively from this description whether or not to rate it important. Whiting and Child used a great many traits where the key variable was the comparativist's judgment on the importance or intensity of the trait. In order to guard against an unconscious bias systematically favoring their hypotheses, they had the traits independently rated by three judges, none of whom knew the hypotheses being tested. The judges were instructed to push their data to the limit, to make inferences (should we call them guesses?) freely from the faintest hints or suggestions, but to rate each judgment for their confidence in it. Whiting and Child systematically evaluated the reliability of these judgments, distinguishing the confident ones from the doubtful ones. Beatrice Whiting, who had access to these ratings before publication, compared her own ratings on importance of sorcery with that of the judges in the Whiting and Child study and found a substantial majority in agreement.

Where the trait studied can only be observed through subjective judgments of comparativists, there is of course nothing else to do but test their reliability as Whiting and Child have done. However, this procedure raises other problems not controlled by them. The procedure measures random error and guards against bias arising from an understanding of the hypothesis being tested and special bias of an individual judge, but it does not guard against other sources of bias—those arising, for example, from the fact that the judges have a common cultural background and may be susceptible to the biases in attitudes of their own culture or, if alerted to this by instruction, may lean over backwards the other way and introduce a systematic overcompensation.

It is far better, I submit, to so define the trait observed that it can be rated by objective criteria independent of the comparativist's judgment. Then the quality control effort can be directed chiefly at the other sources of error in the data collection process: the informant and the ethnographer.

DUTY TO EVALUATE REPORT RELIABILITY

The attitude until now of all English and American exponents of the cross-cultural survey method seems instead to be that of taking printed sources at their face value. At best, perhaps, such manifestly unreliable sources as the accounts of casual tourists are considered unworthy of use; but if a source is used at all, it is used uncritically. This attitude is openly voiced by Homans and Schneider.[5] These writers, in their sensitive and penetrating study of cross-cousin marriage, came across data on the Kaonde and the Kandyu that seemed implausible to them. Nevertheless, possibly motivated by scientific conscientiousness because the data tended to discredit their hypothesis, they decided that "for the sake of consistency we shall abide by our printed sources."

In a trained historian the Homans and Schneider "principle of respecting printed sources" would stimulate strong enthusiasm—enthusiasm fully as warm, say, as that in the breast of a Franz Boas hearing a proposal that henceforth as a matter of principle no anthropologist should ever do field work!

Strange that in the twentieth century it should be necessary to urge the importance of source criticism to a scholarly audience! To give a couple of commonplace historical examples with which I happen to be familiar:

1. None of the printed accounts by participants in the battle of Cedar Creek in the American Civil War can be trusted for a reliable account: the official reports of the com-

manders on either side must be used with great care. Only by a systematic comparison of the dozens of printed accounts of the battle written by participants on both sides can its course be reconstructed.[6]

2. Printed accounts by participants of controversial political events are particularly unreliable; sometimes even two or three independent corroborating statements turn out to be wild distortions. Good examples are the tortured misconceptions of Abraham Lincoln's policy toward the conquered South at the end of the Civil War.[7]

The historian recognizes an obligation to evaluate the reliability of the written documents that constitute his sources of information. The ethnographer recognizes an obligation to evaluate the reliability of statements of informants that likewise often constitute his chief sources of information. The comparativist in a cross-cultural survey has both obligations: the obligation to evaluate the reliability of the ethnographer who writes a field report and the obligation to evaluate the reliability of that ethnographer's informants.

WEAKNESS OF TRADITIONAL SOURCE CRITICISM

Traditional methods of source criticism in historical scholarship can often be extremely powerful.[8] One of the most impressive examples known to me is by Walbank.[9] His study of the life of Aratos of Sicyon draws heavily for its information on classical writers like Livy and Plutarch, who had no firsthand knowledge of the events in question but depended for their information on the now-lost writings of others (including, for example, Aratos' own memoirs). Walbank's study brilliantly evaluates the biases and shortcomings not only of the writers he himself uses but also, by skillful and delicate inference, of the now-lost writers *they* used.

The application of these traditional methods of source criticism to ethnographic writings has been discussed in great detail by Schmidt,[10] an exposition unfortunately associated with the now discredited theoretical framework of the *Kulturkreislehre.* That this application can yield great profits has been demonstrated often, most notably perhaps by the Fuegian studies of Cooper [11] and Gusinde.[12]

Nevertheless, the direct application of these traditional methods to the problem at hand in the manner of Steinmetz and his pupils is risky. These methods all involve subjective evaluations by the investigator. In this involvement lies the trap—a trap which Homans and Schneider seem to have sensed and sought to avoid. If an investigator who is collecting data to test a hypothesis himself applies the subjective judgments of reliability involved in traditional methods of historical source criticism, he is likely to be tempted to reject conflicting data and to accept supporting data. But Homans and Schneider escape this trap only to fall into another: they lean over backwards to accept conflicting data. Either mistake hampers research.

PHILOSOPHY OF INDUSTRIAL PRODUCTION QUALITY CONTROL

To evaluate report reliability, I propose instead to apply the general spirit and philosophy of statistical production quality control, as widely used in industry.[13] The general spirit of such quality control is to test regularly, by sampling methods, the hypothesis that something is seriously wrong with production methods. If the variable tested for (individual dimension, mean, proportion, standard deviation, or range) diverges as much as three standard deviations (sigmas) from the control value, it is ordinarily presumed that something is seriously wrong with production methods and some change is needed. In other words, a *single* error of three sigmas in effect halts production, and tells the production staff they must change their methods.

This control is ordinarily carried out by means of a chart that shows the expected value of the variable and its control limits. Sample values are posted on the chart as a permanent record whose meaning may be seen at a glance by a trained eye. For example, the maker of electrical fuses needs to know that his fuses will melt within a maximum of so many seconds after an overload above the rated electrical current through the fuse. Yet to test a fuse for this quality destroys it. By testing fuses taken at random from his production line, he can see not only the average length of time it takes the sampled fuses to melt but also the spread or range of variation—the variance—from fuse to fuse. By applying the mathematical theory of chance variation, he can see if any special causes or tendencies in the work of production adversely affect the melting time of the fuses. Perhaps the average melting time of the fuses in his sample runs consistently higher than expected. Or perhaps, even though the average melting time is acceptable, the spread or range of variation from fuse to fuse is too great. In either case the laws of chance variation enable the fuse maker to predict that too many of the fuses he has *not* tested will take too long to melt under an overload.

PHILOSOPHY OF DATA QUALITY CONTROL

In data quality control the behavioral scientist working with written records tests indications of unreliability to see if something is seriously wrong with the statements in the records. To be sure, there is an essential difference in the position of the comparativist and the industrial quality control engineer. While both can use analagous methods to detect warnings that something is seriously wrong with the production of electrical fuses or the collection of data on witchcraft, they have dissimilar recourses. If something is wrong with the production of electrical fuses, the production engineer institutes changes in raw materials or production methods and his job is done. True, if something is wrong with the collection of data on witchcraft, the comparativist should likewise recommend changes in the data collection process to future field workers, but to him this is only an incidental response. For the study at hand, his main job is to counteract the effect of the error detected one way or another. Therefore I propose to use the term "control" somewhat more broadly than it is used in industry. By "control of errors" I shall mean not only their detection but also the methods taken to counteract their effect on the results of the study.

In considering data quality control it is essential to distinguish two kinds of errors in data reports: random errors and bias. Random errors occur from carelessness or oversight arising from circumstances that make error in either direction equally likely. Biases occur where factors dispose toward error in one direction rather than the other: biases need not necessarily reflect either the conscious or unconscious desires or preconceptions of the observer, for they can also arise out of the observation situation or the phenomenon being observed.

Ethnographic data, for example, vary greatly in inherent reliability. Some information can be readily collected by casual and untrained travelers: for example, that a people practice agriculture, that they live in long pile-dwellings over the water, that they wear nose-ornaments and color their bodies with paint. Other information—for example, actual sexual behavior that contravenes the mores of the people being studied—generally requires a long stay in the field, excellent rapport with informants, and sophisticated training in eliciting data. In cross-cultural research design, as I have elsewhere pointed out,[14] the ideal practice is to base the hypothesis test on traits that involve easily recognizable criteria about which observers (and informants) tend to agree. However, this kind of research design is not always practical. In the present example, all four tentative indicators of culture stress (protest suicide, defiant homicide, drunken brawling, and alleged witchcraft) constitute violations of Western European mores—and hence of the mores of almost all ethnographers' own cultures. Furthermore, they are sometimes violations of the mores of the people studied (as defiant homicide, by definition, always is). In addition, data on three of the four indicators—all but drunken brawling—must be gathered chiefly by questioning informants rather than by direct observation.

Formal tests of the inherent reliability of data are called for whenever there are available several independent observations of each of a number of examples among the types of phenomena under investigation. One could, for example, compare samples of battle reports in the *Official Records of the Union and Confederate Armies* to sort out the kinds of statements about which observers generally agree. Civil War battle data with a high degree of inherent reliability probably would include dates of battles, names of commanders and units engaged on either side, general location of battles (measured in miles, not in yards), and general character of movements of larger troop units. (For example, on the evening after the battle of Cedar Creek, Sheridan's army remained in possession of the field, while Early's army retreated many miles southward.) The attention of historians however is generally fixed on the inherently unreliable phenomena in this example, statements about which observers often disagree: the exact time of day (to the nearest hour) that a battle starts, the exact movements (to the nearest yard) of smaller troop units (regiments and divisions), the exact statements of this or that general, and—the most hopelessly unreliable of phenomena—his *reasons* for making this or that decision.

The philosophy of data quality control, then, is simple. Field reports are classified by conditions of observation. Circumstances are selected that seem likely to affect the reliability of field reports and to produce either random error or systematic bias. Those reports gathered under supposedly more favorable conditions are accordingly called "favorable reports"; those under supposedly less favorable conditions, "unfavorable reports." Statistical tests are made to see if there is a statistically significant difference between favorable and unfavorable reports. Thus, for example, the investigator tests to see if favorable reports are more likely to report high rates of suicide than unfavorable reports. If the test fails to reveal a statistically significant difference, the data are considered reliable and the data collection process is considered in working control. Of course, if the circumstances of observation selected as control factors do not in fact affect the reports as supposed, this might well also explain an absence of a statistically significant difference. Where, however, a statistically significant difference occurs in reports on some traits but not on others (for example, where it occurs in reports on witchcraft attribution but not in reports on drunken brawling, as in this study), the quality control procedure itself is provisionally validated along with the reliability of the reports on the second trait.

The present study uses six main control factors in the general data quality control tests (see Chapters 4 and 7): (1) collection of specific case reports by the ethnographer, (2) use by the ethnographer of direct observation and personal participation in an ongoing culture as a major source of field data, (3) length of stay in the field among the people studied by the ethnographer, (4) familiarity of the ethnographer with the language of the people studied, (5) role of the ethnographer among the people studied (such as, social scientist, missionary, government official), and (6) explicitness and generality of the ethnographer's report on the trait in question, with the concomitant presence or absence of a need for inference by the comparativist in order to classify the report. These control factors were chosen intuitively, from judgments made after the present writer's own field experience both as an intelligence officer in Germany in 1945 and as a social anthropologist in the Tyrol in 1956. The writer's judgments were also influenced by his training in traditional methods of source criticism as generally used by professional historians today. The control factors are all widely supported by the general opinion of the anthropological profession in the United States today. But of course authoritative professional opinion often errs and is no substitute for empirical test.

VALIDATION OF CONTROL FACTORS

In this study two control factors receive provisional validation—Control Factor 3, length of stay, and Control Factor 6, explicitness and generality of reports. I assert that these factors are provisionally validated because I find in fact a statistically significant relationship between each of these factors on one hand and a set of trait reports on the other: Factor 3 is validated as to witchcraft attribution and Factor 6 as to protest suicide. Theoretically, of course, each of these relationships might be artifacts of some other factor: sampling bias, since the Human Relations Area Files are a judgmental rather than a random sample; unit definition differences, since the social unit constituting a "society" for the purposes of the Files is nowhere defined and there is no claim of consistency in defining these units; historical association, since the traits studied may have diffused throughout certain regions which in turn have been studied by ethnographers from a single culture; and so on. Correlation does not prove causation, and so I have not incontrovertibly nor finally demonstrated the validity of these factors. I have not demonstrated that the association of high witchcraft attribution reports with long-staying ethnographers reflects the success of informants at deceiving short-staying ethnographers by denying witchcraft attribution. Nevertheless, I submit that, when one considers specific case data documenting such deception by the Navahos (Clyde Kluckhohn) and by several Indian peoples of Mexico (Ralph Beals), no other explanation of this correlation is nearly as plausible. Similarly, I have not finally demonstrated that the correlation between explicitness and generality of suicide reports and their classification by me reflects a classification bias on my part; nevertheless, I submit that this is clearly the most plausible explanation.

But it is important to remember that it does not matter to us very much whether or not we understand correctly the association of reporting conditions and traits reported. It does not matter to us very much whether we are right or wrong.

We may be right. Long-stayers may tend to report high witchcraft attribution because they are less likely to be imposed upon by lying informants and thus more likely to make trustworthy reports. But short-stayers may tend to report low witchcraft attribution because they are more likely to be imposed upon by lying informants and thus less likely to make trustworthy reports.

We may be wrong. Long-stayers may tend to report high witchcraft attribution because of some defect in their character that also makes them compulsively remain in the field while short-stayers may be able, efficient workers who get the job done quickly, get it done accurately, and go home.

Assume for the sake of argument that something of this sort goes on, that it is the *short-stayers* who make the trustworthy reports and the *long-stayers* who make the untrustworthy reports. What is the effect of such a situation upon the validity of our quality control procedure? *None!* The purpose of data quality control is not to study the reporting conditions for their own sake but to control bias in correlations among the traits being reported. If it is the long-stayers who make the errors and the short-stayers who report accurately, the problem of bias producing spurious correlations remains the same. We wish to see whether correlations between traits being studied are artifacts of reporting conditions. To do this, we correlate each trait with each data quality control indicator: if one trait in a correlation proves related to the reporting conditions, we retain partial control; but if both traits prove so related, the correlation is out of control and partial analysis to allow for the influence of the reporting condition is mandatory. We proceed in just the same way to control for errors in reports related to length of stay whether the errors tend to be made by the long-stayers or by the short-stayers. It does not matter which, and we do not have to know which.

We may be wrong in another way. The association we have detected between length of stay and witchcraft attribution reports may not reflect any reporting bias at all. Conceivably, societies that have high witchcraft attribution rates might attract anthropologists to stay longer to study them. If this were so, neither long-stayers nor short-stayers might tend to make reporting errors; their stay might simply be a function of the trait being studied, or some other trait related to it. What is the effect of such a situation upon the validity of our control procedure? Again, *none!* If the foregoing assumption is correct, reporting biases related to length of stay do not exist, but only seem to. Consequently, the correlations in the traits we are really interested in cannot be spurious, cannot be mere artifacts of reporting bias. If such a situation holds, our control procedures are not invalid; they are merely unnecessary.

To sum up, we validate control factors only provisionally; these tests do not establish finally that reporting biases of the sort presumed, or even any reporting biases at all, actually exist. However, when a control factor is validated, it creates a presumption of need for its use, to guard against the possibility of a reporting bias. If it is used in the manner here proposed, that possibility is effectively guarded against.

CONTROL OF RANDOM ERROR

The great danger from random errors is that they may prevent the investigator from confirming the existence of relationships which do in fact exist. For example, if the true correlation is high, random errors will most likely tend to lower the correlation in the observations. Consider the typical fourfold test of association between, say, matrilineal descent and matrilocal residence rules. Assume that in fact these two are highly correlated but that in the course of collecting data on them, random errors are made by informants, field workers, and the investigator in a cross-cultural survey. Since the two variables are highly correlated, there are many more favorable cases than unfavorable; consequently, informants, field workers, and comparativists are more likely through random error to change a favorable case to an unfavorable one than vice versa.

On the other hand, consider two other variables which are utterly unrelated. There are an equal number of favorable and unfavorable cases. Random error is likely to change about as many favorable to unfavorable as vice versa, leaving the final result the same. Furthermore—and this is

very important—the probability that through chance a correlation will be produced because more unfavorable cases
are changed to favorable than vice versa is congruent with
the probability that a like result will occur from random
sampling error. The calculus of probability normally applied
to test the significance of correlations measures the likelihood
of such an occurrence.

Consequently, as Driver [15] has pointed out, if a cross-cultural survey reports a statistically significant correlation, the
more random errors are detected in data processing, the
higher the true correlation is likely to be. Statistically significant correlations are observed *in spite* of random errors,
not because of them.

So it may often happen that no counteracting efforts are
needed. If random error is detected but the hypothesis
studied is nevertheless confirmed, the comparativist is justified in concluding that the true relationship is even stronger
than that observed. If, however, the hypothesis studied is
not confirmed and the comparativist believes this failure is
due to random error—for example, if correlations are in the
direction predicted and nearly but not quite statistically
significant—he can control the effect of random error by
making a study of a *new* sample in which he systematically
eliminates the data from observations made under less
favorable conditions. If random error has lowered true
correlations substantially, this procedure can be expected
to raise them. A pilot study searching for indications of
random error might be the most efficient procedure.

However, it is essential that the classification of observations into those made under more and less favorable conditions be based on purely objective criteria, and that the
comparativist's judgment be entirely excluded from the
process. Otherwise, his biases may intrude. A method for

accomplishing this classification, the observation quality index, will be described in detail and illustrated by application later in this work.

CONTROL OF BIAS

Bias needs to be dealt with quite differently from random error. If bias is detected in the observations on one of the variables in a study, the key question is the presence and nature of a related bias in other variables hypothetically correlated with the first. If there is a related bias, it can systematically destroy the evidence that a correlation exists when in fact it does, or it can systematically produce evidence that a correlation exists when in fact it does not.

For example, in the quality control tests on suicide data below, evidence turned up suggests the possibility that reports by observers unfamiliar with the native language and/or not practicing participant observation of an ongoing culture may tend to consistently underestimate suicide rates. Let us assume for the moment that this bias is confirmed by later studies. What would its effect be on a test of culture stress theory seeking correlations between causes and symptoms? If no bias exists in the reports of these kinds of observers on causes of culture stress, little harm will have been done. Perhaps a few borderline cases will be changed from high suicide to low suicide, with results analogous to those of a random error among those few cases (since there will be a random choice of associated culture stress cause). Unless the bias is very strong in its effect (a hypothesis the present study fails to support), it can safely be overlooked.

But suppose that these kinds of observers also have a bias in their reports on hypothetical causes of culture stress. Suppose, for example, that they consistently underestimate frequency of starvation or of sexual frustrations. Then a spurious correlation will tend to result, indicating an association between low suicide rates and absence of starvation or absence of sexual frustration. Such a correlation would seem to support the culture stress hypothesis when in fact it merely reflects observational errors. Or if the bias were in the opposite direction, it would systematically destroy evidence of true correlation which in fact existed.

THE CONCEPT OF WORKING CONTROL

A key concept of data quality control is the concept of working control. This concept sees data quality control tests as a systematic search for indications of danger in the data collection process. Where this search reveals statistically significant evidence of danger, the investigator concludes that something is seriously wrong with that process and some steps need to be taken to deal with the danger. This is basically the concept of industrial statistical quality control.

As used in industry, quality control tests usually call for significance at the 0.0023 level (three standard deviations). If a result that unusual occurs, the control engineer presumes that something is wrong with the production process, that it is out of control. If, however, the tests fail to produce a result that unusual, then the production process is considered to be in working control and it is assumed that the product quality is acceptable.

Applying this concept to data quality control would call for systematic testing of data for bias, as demonstrated in Chapter 4 of this work. As long as no evidence of bias significant at the level indicated turns up, the data collection process can be considered in working control and hence the data can be considered acceptable. Where evidence of bias significant at the level indicated does turn up, this halts the data collection process; a presumption of bias is established, and steps are called for to guard against intrusion of this bias into the research conclusions.

The use of this method would be even more reassuring if sequential statistical tests were used [16] instead of the conventional tests of significance as used here. This is so because a sequential test decides between *two* alternative hypotheses. For data quality control work, one hypothesis might be that there is no bias, the other that there is bias of a stated degree. Where a sequential test of like power is used to test the substantive hypotheses of the study, it seems intuitively satisfying if the substantive hypothesis is validated by the sequential tests while the data collection bias hypothesis is rejected.

The concept of working control as here proposed makes the observations classed as "favorable" the measure of the existence of bias in the observations classed as "unfavorable." This involves a fundamental difference from the philosophy of industrial quality control, which makes the characteristics of products chosen for inspection by random sampling a measure of the characteristics of products not inspected. It will be seen that the validity of data quality control depends upon this classification of observation conditions as "favorable" or "unfavorable." However, each separate quality control test stands on its own feet in this regard. In the present study, for example, we conclude that Test 5 probably lacks validity; that Tests 1 and 2 have conflicting results and consequently the validity of at least one of them is doubtful; but that the validity of Tests 3 and 6 is strongly supported by this study, while that of Test 4 is likewise supported, although weakly.

The initial application of a data quality control test is then necessarily tentative and this study is essentially an exploratory one. Where control factors are empirically validated, as Factors 3 and 6 are in this study, their use in future studies of the traits relevant to which they are validated becomes mandatory—and in future studies of any other traits, strongly indicated. Where no significant relationship appears to exist between the control factors and a trait being controlled, as is here the case with drunken brawling reports, the trait reports are to be treated as in working control; for this result affords the investigator the intuitively satisfying assurance that data collected under conditions generally considered favorable do not differ as a class from those collected under conditions generally considered unfavorable. In other words, if he has confidence in correlations based on field reports collected by professional anthropologists who assemble specific case data as well as generalizations, who report an ongoing way of life in which they directly participate as much as they can, who stay a year or more in the field, who learn the native language, and who report their findings explicitly and state that they are applicable to the whole society studied—if reports like these seem to him fit to be trusted in scientific research then this battery of quality control tests shows that he likewise can put his trust in correlations based on reports of drunken brawling that *lack* these characteristics. This then is what is implied by the concept of working control as used here.

TREATMENT OF BIASED TRAITS

Where the data quality control tests produce evidence of bias, the data collection process is presumed to be partly out of control. (In the present study, the sample was small and the tests used not very sensitive; consequently in the discussion of the tests in Chapter 7, I have taken pains to point out suggestions of bias even where they do not attain statistical significance.) What then needs to be done about it?

First, the investigator in his own mind classes these reports as biased and reports them as such.

Second, the investigator carefully tests for like bias any of the traits hypothetically associated with the biased trait in order to protect his study from spurious correlations reflecting data collection bias. Only where like bias occurs in a hypothetically correlated trait is the research process wholly out of control. As has already been indicated, if one is investigating the hypothesis that frequency of warfare is associated with witchcraft attribution, the substantive test to be controlled is the test for correlation between societies with frequent wars and societies with high witchcraft attribution rates. Assume that witchcraft attribution reports are biased to reflect length of stay of ethnographer, but that warfare reports are not so biased. Then a certain number of societies who really have high witchcraft attribution rates will be erroneously reported as having low witchcraft attribution rates by ethnographers who stayed only a short time in the field. However, these ethnographers *ex hypothesi* are unbiased reporters of warfare frequency. Either the hypothesis being tested is valid or it is not. If valid, then more often than not high rates of witchcraft attribution are in fact associated with high frequences of warfare, but our short-term anthropologists will tend to report many of these erroneously as cases of low witchcraft attribution associated with frequent warfare. The effect of these errors will be to produce a reported correlation *lower* than the true one. If the hypothesis being tested is not valid, then high witchcraft attribution rates are as likely to be associated with low frequencies of warfare as with high frequencies; the biased reporting errors are as likely to change a case which in fact has an association of the predicted sort to one which does not as vice versa. Thus if there is in fact no correlation between the traits, the bias will not tend to report one; if there is in fact a correlation, the stronger the bias, the lower the correlation that is likely to be reported. Such a bias then has the same effect as random error in tending to destroy evidence of relationship but not to manufacture a spurious correlation.

But let us now assume a different case: that short-staying anthropologists are not only likely to underestimate the importance of witchcraft attribution but also are likely to underestimate the frequency of warfare. That is to say, let us now assume that warfare reports have a bias parallel to witchcraft attribution reports. The data collection process is now wholly out of control, for this bias could well produce a spurious correlation between frequency of warfare and importance of witchcraft attribution even if in fact these traits were entirely unrelated. A study which purported to discover important relationships among social and cultural behavior of the societies studied might, in fact, be only reflecting distortions of data made by ethnographers.

Where both traits being investigated have a reporting bias and hence are wholly out of control, the investigator needs to treat this reporting bias as a causal factor in his statistical analysis. His analysis in effect is of reports and he wishes to enquire whether reports known to be influenced by reporting conditions are also influenced by the behavior of the people reported on. In short, when reports are wholly out of control, the investigator has a problem of partial correlation, or of analysis of variance, or of covariance, or of partial association, depending upon the form of his data.[17]

In one sense, of course, the definition of working control is entirely arbitrary: like all other statistical inference using probability theory, it depends upon an arbitrarily specified significance level. The significance level is of course the measure of the likelihood of a similar result occurring through chance in a random sample from a universe in which no relationship of the sort investigated exists. (Some statistical purists would prefer us to restrict the use of statistical inference to inference about universes made from rigorously random samples. But investigators whose chief interest is social science rather than mathematics are often interested in the likelihood of a similar result occurring through chance from a random sample from a universe in which no relationship of the sort investigated exists, even when they know well that the data in question are not a random sample or even a sample at all! They want to know if this is the sort of thing you would expect to get by chance.) It specifies a probability of the investigator being deceived by a freak sample.

In industrial quality control, the control limit is usually set at three standard deviations, as we have noted; this means that if in fact nothing is wrong with the production process, and the sample is strictly random, sampling freaks are on the average going to mislead the investigator less than three times in every thousand samples. At whatever degree the significance level is set, as long as it is explicit both the investigator and the reader of the report know where they stand. Both will of course be keenly interested in comparing significance levels used in data quality control with significance levels used in accepting the substantive hypotheses being studied.

APPLICATION TO OTHER DISCIPLINES

This work applies data quality control to ethnographic data. Most of its control factors are characteristically applicable to the ethnographic data collection process and may be of little use in controlling other kinds of data reports. To apply this technique to other kinds of written reports, one must begin by classifying the reports according to what one presumes are the favorable and unfavorable observation conditions. To perform this first step effectively, one must of course be familiar with the kind of document in question, the conditions of its compilation and the kind of information about those conditions which is likely to be available.

To illustrate how data quality control might be applied to historiography, let me suggest a number of control factors which might well be used in evaluating reports about the behavior of the Union and Confederate Armies in the American Civil War:

1. Time lapse between event reported and recording of report. The *Official Records* [18] contain many reports or action messages written on the spot at the time. Many letters home and diaries of participants are available, and many reports by journalists are also available. Many of these constitute records made during or very soon after the occurrence of the events recorded. On the other hand, the formal reports on actions by unit commanders in the *Official Records* as well as the memoirs of participants were mostly written months or years after.

2. Professional stake of author in report. While few reporters of Civil War battles were unconcerned with the outcome, concern varied greatly from that of a general with his reputation to defend to that of an enlisted man like De Forest with an aloof view of leadership on both sides.

3. Agreement or disagreement by authors with opposing viewpoints. Many important events of the Civil War are described (as in *Battles and Leaders* [19]) by generals who commanded opposing armies and whose viewpoints and biases often directly conflict. Similarly, we have accounts of administrative problems not only by Union and Confederate officials with similar roles but also by civilian and military officials—by the general being supplied and by the cabinet minister supplying him.

4. Proximity of author to event recorded. Some records themselves constitute events—for example, the spurious decoy dispatch from Longstreet to Early which was intended

to deceive Sheridan.[20] Some records are made by persons who directly participated in the immediate event concerned. Some records are made by those who, though not themselves participants, themselves witnessed the event. Some records are made by those who, though neither participants nor eyewitnesses, received verbal reports of the event at the time, reports not otherwise recorded.

5. Intensity of involvement of author and event recorded. Some authors were more deeply and intimately involved in a given event than others, thus presumably reacted more intensely to it.

6. Military experience of author. For certain kinds of events, technical military training and experience would presumably better qualify an author to observe, remember and record accurately.

7. Explicitness of report. Some reports are couched in language requiring no inference or interpretation by the investigator; others require inference or interpretation—here the bias of the investigator can intrude.

The value of these control factors can only be shown by a thorough study of the sources on the American Civil War, a study beyond the scope of the present work. Whether these or similar factors might not be used with equal practicality and validity in studies of other wars would depend upon the corpus of records surviving as well as on the nature of the conflict, and could only be determined by further study.

But it must be emphasized that this method is applicable to qualitative data as well as quantitative. The statistics involved are applied to counts of instances of reports of this or that sort of event collected in this or that sort of way. This technique is similar to content analysis [21] and, like it, counts statements of kinds defined in advance and treats these counts statistically.

CROCE'S PROBLEM

In the last few decades, the opinion has spread among professional historians that selection bias constitutes an insuperable barrier to scientific historiography.[22] The pervasive role of selection bias in historical science has been most eloquently and insistently expressed by Benedetto Croce.[23] Since the corpus of events which occur in all their richness of detail is beyond the scope of any possible effort to record completely, all basic historical records are selections from these events which reflect the bias of the record maker. Furthermore, even the corpus of basic records—original sources—is far too detailed where many periods of history are concerned to permit the compiler of historical studies to present all the data there—he too intrudes a selection bias since he must choose what data he considers important and hence worthy of attention. Finally, in any scientific study, the selection of the problem itself reflects the bias of the investigator's personal interest.

As long as historiography remains a form of belles-lettres in which the attention given to a topic is unhampered by any discipline—as long as historiography keeps its present form—these problems would seem indeed insuperable. Where however the historical inquiry is transformed into a quantitative study the data selection biases can be controlled by data quality control.

I. Selection Bias in Basic Sources

Here the problem is to control the omission of information on key traits. Assume that a study, not controlling for this bias, reports a correlation between two traits—for example, between size of largest settlement and frequency of warfare. The Crocean hypothesis would be that this correlation may be an artifact of selection bias, in that only those societies in which large settlements are associated with frequent warfare or small settlements with infrequent warfare tend to keep records of these traits while those societies in which large settlements are associated with infrequent warfare or small settlements are associated with frequent warfare tend not to keep records of those traits. If such a bias indeed exists, two control traits come to mind which could be expected to detect it:

a. Copiousness of records kept by the society during a given period. If the bias is a casual and unconscious one, this test should reveal it, since where more copious records are kept, these particular data, considered less important by the record keepers *ex hypothesi,* would be more likely to turn up.

b. Descriptions by foreign observers (for example, diplomatic correspondence, missionary or travelers' accounts). If a people are consciously and deliberately suppressing records of the data in question, this test should reveal it, since foreigners writing for their own people would escape the influence of the prohibition.

2. Selection Bias in Secondary Works

If feasible, a correlational study should avoid the use of secondary works and prefer the use of primary sources. Certainly a major proportion of its data should be drawn from primary sources. It then becomes a simple matter to control for selection bias in secondary works by using source proximity as a control factor. In this study, Control Factor 2 provides such a test of the ethnographic sources here used. In general, the topic of source proximity needs more attention. In a recent paper, Pierce [24] has proposed that primary and secondary sources be classified further according to the authenticity of the text actually examined: whether original manuscript, transcription, translation and so on. For data quality control purposes, it would seem more important to subdivide the traditional concepts of primary and secondary sources. I propose a six-level classification:

Primary Sources

a. DATUM REPORT: Where an artifact or a statement is itself the trait being studied. Studies of material culture which examine specimens of the artifacts in question, studies of folk-tale distributions which examine texts of the tales in question, studies of constitutional theory which examine texts of formal written constitutions have direct access to the trait being studied. The comparativist can himself examine the trait without dependence upon informant or native record-maker or ethnographer or historiographer.

b. PARTICIPANT REPORT: Where an event or culture pattern is described by a participating culture bearer. Native scholars' accounts in ethnography, memoirs or diaries by participants in historiography constitute a general class of such reports. Where records of individual events or of defunct culture patterns are in question, the lapse of time between the occurrence of the event or pattern and the compilation of the record is a factor which needs to be seriously considered.

c. OBSERVER'S REPORT: Where an event or culture pattern is described by an eyewitness who is not himself a participant in the culture or subculture pattern involved. So-called participant-observation ethnographies usually fall into this class as to much of the routine of daily life in the society described. For civil war battles, we would class accounts by soldiers or officials themselves as participant reports but accounts by journalists who witness events as observers' reports.

d. DERIVATIVE REPORT: An account by a nonobserver based on a report of another which no longer is available for·study, thus making the derivative report the primary source of information on the event or culture pattern in question. In ethnography, field notes on informants' statements acquire this status when the informant dies, as do ethnographic reports by the ethnographer based on his field notes and his memory of his informants' statements. Many basic records in record-keeping societies likewise fall into this class: accounts obtained by questioning eyewitnesses or participants and recorded by a journalist, for example. Finally, secondary works based on primary sources that have since been lost fall into this class: Plutarch's life of Aratus of Sicyon, for example, is based largely on Aratus' memoirs, which now are lost. Since this category contains several subclasses with important differences, it may in some studies be convenient to subclassify it still further. It might be valuable, for instance, to give attention to the conditions in which the author of the derivative report worked, the evidence for the presence or absence of a critical attitude of his toward his sources, and so on.

Secondary Sources

e. SCHOLAR'S REPORT: An account by a nonobserver, based on existing primary sources which the comparativist does not find it convenient to consult directly, that cites the specific passages in these sources on which the scholar relies for his statements about the data in question.

f. READER'S REPORT: An account by a nonobserver based on other writings, in which specific passages in primary sources covering the data in question are not cited. Such works often lean heavily on other secondary sources for their data.

THE SELECTION OF THE PROBLEM

At least two criteria suggest themselves by which the choice of problems can be evaluated objectively. The first of these is the generality and elegance of the hypothesis being tested. Theories of social and cultural evolution, for example, purport to reduce much of human affairs to a few simple principles, as for that matter do the theories of a great many quacks and cranks. Now if a man says that all social problems reflect simply the phases of the moon, you are justified in questioning his evidence most skeptically and in the absence of a plausible demonstration dismissing him as a crank—*but* his problem is a valid one, since it purports to reduce social science to a simple principle. The selection of the problem is only one step in the scientific research process and untrained thinkers are likely to be led into folly by their ignorance of the remaining steps. In practice, we ask also for some evidence that an investigator is aware of scientific research discipline—a competent research report being, of course, itself the best evidence on this point. Assuming such competence, however, the more general and elegant in form the hypothesis being tested, the more important and valuable the problem. Certainly as to successful research studies, which validate the hypothesis being investigated as substantially as current research methods permit, we can say without hesitation that the generality and elegance of the hypothesis tested is an objective measure of the validity of the effort of investigating it at all.

A second criterion that might be used to evaluate the selection of a research problem is its relevance to pressing social, economic or other cultural problems faced by the society in which the investigator works—this is the criterion of practicality. While dedicated scientists generally would prefer a problem important by the first criterion, the second criterion obviously also has its place.

Other criteria of evaluation may well exist; I mention only these simply to make the point that there are obvious ways to evaluate the selection of social science research topics. It is true that neither of these criteria are relevant to the problem of the historian who with Leopold von Ranke seeks not to instruct but merely to tell how things happened. Ranke's task remains an art, not a science. I submit that we can use data quality control together with other needed techniques to do comparative statistical studies modeled on the cross-cultural survey which uncover and demonstrate laws of history. What one cannot do scientifically is to achieve Ranke's aim: *"Ich will bloss sagen, wie es eigentlich gewesen."*

SPECIAL SITUATIONS

The main emphasis of this work is on the general data quality control in Chapters 4 and 7 of the culture stress symptoms discussed in Chapters 2 and 3. However, as already indicated, two special problems in data quality control are involved in dealing with quantitative rate reports such as those here connected with protest suicide and defiant homicide. The first of these is the problem of evaluating random error resulting from extrapolation of rates from small populations: this problem is dealt with in Chapter 5. The second is the problem of the reliability of the population estimates from which rates are computed: this problem is dealt with in Chapter 6. Both of these special situations involve treatment of the problem of random error; that of Chapter 6 also considers the possibility of bias in certain kinds of population reports. Consequently, although not essential to the general presentation of data quality control, they constitute useful and pertinent supplements, and are required for the full evaluation of the reliability of the defiant homicide and protest suicide reports collected and discussed in Chapter 7.

IMPORTANCE OF TRAIT DEFINITION

As will be seen in Chapter 4, control of the third stage of the data collection process involves comparison of reports in which the judgment and inferences of the comparativist play a part in the classification with those in which they do not. In order for there to be any reports of the latter kind, it is necessary for the traits to be so clearly and rigorously defined that a detailed and explicit and generalized report in effect classifies itself. The construction of clear and rigorous definitions of the traits being classified is the main task of Chapter 3.

RELEVANCE OF CULTURE STRESS THEORY

To illustrate the application of statistical data quality control to a research problem in which the detection of bias is a critical element in the research design, this report turns to a consideration of culture stress theory.

CHAPTER 2

Some Problems in Culture Stress Research

IMPORTANCE OF CULTURE STRESS RESEARCH

Progress in research on culture stress brings with it not only progress in research on mental health but also progress in research on the scientific evaluation of culture.

It is widely believed that variations in culture stress cause variations in mental illness rates. True, the accurate determination of the prevalance of mental illness in a community by the census method is an extremely exacting and expensive undertaking. Nevertheless, nearly a dozen such studies have been made in a number of different cultures, and their results [1] show that wide variations in mental illness rates from culture to culture undoubtedly occur. The question remains whether such variations in mental illness rates might not reflect other factors than cultural stress—factors such as differences in climate or diet or body chemistry—which, while not perceived as painful by the individual, nevertheless produce mental illness. For while the theory of culture

37

stress is widely held today, it has never been rigorously tested. There are no well-established indicators of culture stress.

A rigorous test of the theory of culture stress might thus shed much light on the causes of mental illness. Such a test might also have a by-product of the first importance. A valid measure of culture stress would have profound moral and philosophical implications, extending beyond the field of mental health. In 1947, the American Anthropological Association officially reported that as yet no scientific means has been found to evaluate cultures.[2] This report expressed the widespread philosophy of cultural relativity, so eloquently stated by Ruth Benedict.[3] But a valid measure of cultural stress might provide an objective yardstick for evaluating cultures scientifically from the viewpoint of their effect upon the individuals who hear them. Of course, other yardsticks might also be developed with differing results. It might be true that from the point of view of an outside observer, some kinds and degrees of culture stress might be invigorating to a society and might make it more likely to survive in a competitive struggle for existence with another society with a lower level of stress. But at least we could say that other things being equal, the lower the culture stress level, the better a society it is for the individual member to live in, as long as it lasts.

CONCEPT OF CULTURE STRESS

In recent decades the opinion has spread among social scientists and psychiatrists that cultures differ importantly in the degree to which they put stress on their culture bearers, on the people who follow their patterns.[4] As the Arsenians put it, some cultures are "tough" on their people, others are "easy." The basic concept of culture stress used here is that in every culture demands are made on the individual which he perceives as painful and from his personal point of view undesirable. The demands may be commands or prohibitions, demands to do or suffer something unpleasant or demands to refrain from doing or enjoying something pleasant. To him as an individual such demands may be hurtful—even though they may benefit the society to which he belongs and some or all of the other individuals which make it up.

This concept of stress takes into consideration the fact that culture is among other things a system of interacting with the environment, of affording benefits to individuals, protecting them from injuries and helping and comforting them when in trouble. To a large extent the culture affects the risks the individual runs as well as the benefits he enjoys. Consequently, in measuring the effect of culture upon the individual, I consider what culture fails to do *for* him as well as what it does *to* him. I consider the stress of hunger or illness as culture stress even though both are primarily physiological problems. This concept of culture stress considers the total way of life, including all the environmental factors of climate, natural resources, communicable disease, accidental injuries and so on. From the point of view of the individual, the culture should take care of these things, or should train him to take care of them himself.

VALIDATION OF CULTURE STRESS THEORY

Are some cultures in fact harder on their people than others? Are avoidable cultural pressures a basic factor in mental illness? Are some ways of life hence better to follow than others? One of the most impressive answers anthropology could give to these questions would be a rigorous cross-cultural survey seeking correlations between hypothesized causes of culture stress and hypothesized symptoms. For such a study, various sorts of hypothesized causes and various sorts of hypothesized symptoms should be included. An ideally successful test would show positive correlations between each of the tested causes and each of the tested symptoms.[5] Such a result would logically establish the theory of culture stress as a scientifically validated working hypothesis. It is true that correlations do not prove causation. But as Karl Popper[6] points out, all scientific generalizations are tentative. While the reasoning that leads to a scientific study or experiment may be inductive, the logic of the research test itself is deductive. A scientific hypothesis is logically examined, and from it the largest possible number of empirically refutable statements are deduced. These refutable statements are systematically tested by observation. If any statement which necessarily follows from the theory is refuted by observation, the theory is refuted. Scientists can never prove conclusively the truth of correct theories but they can often conclusively disprove incorrect theories. Scientific research is a continuing effort to do the latter. Murdock[7] has shown by large-scale application the usefulness in anthropological cross-cultural surveys of this logical approach, which he styles the method of postulates.

The Study by Whiting and Child

But formidable problems of method still weaken any cross-cultural survey test of cultural stress theory. The difficulties to be overcome can best be appreciated by a critique of the important study by Whiting and Child.[8] Although these investigators were not interested in the general problem of culture stress as such but instead were testing theories of the effect of certain child training practices on adult personality, their work constitutes the most rigorous test of culture stress theory so far. They considered in effect the severity or mildness of stress in weaning, toilet training, and indoctrination in proper sexual, dependence, and aggression behavior. These factors they correlated with various kinds of explanations of illness and various kinds of therapies of illness.

However, the Whiting and Child study has four major weaknesses:

1. The child-training practices which seem to be among the causes of culture stress are not readily researchable through library study at present. Data from existing ethnological literature is too sparse and unreliable.[9] As Whiting and Child frankly admit:

We did not wish to have the judge [who was rating the cultures for the traits studied by reading the available literature] make only those judgments which he could make with a high degree of confidence; the number of cases might then be reduced to a number too small for use, whereas the doubtful judgments might have enough evidence behind them to yield meaningful results with the larger number of cases that would then be available.[10]

In defense of Whiting and Child, it should be noted that as discussed in detail later in this paper, the more random errors which their procedure introduced into their work, the *higher* must the true correlations in the universe be, since despite these random errors statistically significant correlations were observed. However, systematic bias resulting either from systematic errors in the literature or in the judges' ratings might logically be a source of spurious correlations and thus invalidate their results.

2. The statistical measures used (t test for significance of difference between means [11] and coefficent of correlation [12]) assume normality of distribution.[13] Three alternative courses of action can meet this difficulty: (a) the investigator can consider the shape of the distributions used to see whether they depart importantly from normality; or (b) he can use some kind of transformation which normalizes them; or (c)

like Murdock,[14] he can use nonparametric statistics—those that make no assumptions about normality of distribution.[15] But Whiting and Child did none of these.

3. Though the statistical methods used assume random sampling, the sample of societies was not truly random but rather judgmental.[16] No method is yet known for random sampling of cultures. For one thing there is no agreement on the definition of the unit of study.[17] For another, most of the known cultures have too little information to be studied if sampled.[18] Finally there is no complete list of world cultures to sample from (although Murdock [19] is nearly complete, and the omitted cultures are chiefly those about which little is known).

4. There is no satisfactory evidence that the cases are historically independent. The test is for functional association—association of child training practices with explanations and treatments of illness which are thought to arise from the nature of human culture and personality. But there is no assurance that the observed correlations do not instead merely reflect historical accidents of the spread of culture patterns through borrowing or migration. I am elsewhere presenting two methods for the solution of this problem, which is widely discussed in the literature on the cross-cultural survey method.[20]

The present work deals with the first problem—that of discerning reliable data on culture stress in existing ethnological literature. But any rigorous test of the theory of culture stress also requires solution of two others: historical independence and random sampling.

The Problem of Cultural Context

The problem of cultural context is another often mentioned difficulty about comparisons in cultural anthropology, although it is usually brought up about old-fashioned comparative studies of the Comtean school rather than modern comparative studies of the cross-cultural survey type. The old-fashioned studies, of which the best known example is Frazer,[21] have often been properly criticized for ignoring the cultural context of the traits they studied. As Ruth Benedict put it a quarter of a century ago:

> Studies of culture like *The Golden Bough* and the usual comparative ethnological volumes are analytical discussions of traits and ignore all the aspects of cultural integration. Mating or death practices are illustrated by bits of behavior selected indiscriminately from the most different cultures, and the discussion builds up a kind of mechanical Frankenstein's monster with a right eye from Fiji, a left from Europe, one leg from Tierra del Fuego, and one from Tahiti, and all the fingers and toes from still different regions. Such a figure corresponds to no reality in the past or present, and the fundamental difficulty is the same as if, let us say, psychiatry ended with a catalogue of the symbols of which psychopathic individuals make use, and ignored the study of patterns of symptomatic behavior—schizophrenia, hysteria, and manic-depressive disorders—into which they are built. The role of the trait in the behavior of the psychotic, the degree to which it is dynamic in the total personality, and its relation to all other items of experience, differ completely. If we are interested in mental processes, we can satisfy ourselves only by relating the particular symbol to the total configuration of the individual.[22]

It is true that the cross-cultural survey by its nature cannot construct such a Frankenstein's monster. The cross-cultural survey compares the relationship between elements of configurations—it compares, so to speak, the brain weight-body weight ratio of a man from Fiji with that of a man from Europe, a man from Tierra del Fuego, a man from Tahiti, and of other men from still different regions. It is in fact a statistical study of cultural context.

However, even in the cross-cultural survey, the investigator must still take care that his categories are culture-free—that is, generally applicable and equally meaningful in any cultural or historical context. He must avoid taking a special category relevant only in some cultures. Fortunately, as Murdock [23] pointed out, all human cultures are built on a single basic cultural plan, just as all mammals are built on a single basic anatomical plan; all human cultures share many scores of trait categories: all have nuclear families, kinship terminologies, incest rules, division of labor, and so on. The investigator can validly compare physiologically a nose of a man from Fiji not only with that of a man from Europe or Tierra del Fuego, but also with that of a cat, a bat, or a rat. However, in making these comparisons, he needs to be aware of the range of function—of variations in keenness of sense of smell, both absolutely and relatively to keenness of other sense organs. He needs also to be aware of the variation in importance (among people at least, and perhaps also among other mammals) of various shapes of noses as they affect mating choices—a variation which among people is often culturally determined. In order to avoid violations of cultural context, then, it is not enough that the investigator systematically compare the relationship of one element of a cultural configuration with another element in the same configuration. He must also so define his elements that his categories of comparison are equally applicable in all human cultures, and he must be aware of the range of variations of form and function that occur among the specific instances of his categories. However, a category which is appropriate for describing behavior in a single cultural context may not prove appropriate for describing the same behavior at the higher level of abstraction used in comparative studies. Goodenough says:

. . . what we do as ethnographers is, and must be kept, independent of what we do as comparative ethnologists. An ethnographer is constructing a theory that will make intelligible what goes on in a particular social universe. A comparativist is trying to find principles common to many different universes. His data are not the direct observations of an ethnographer, but the laws governing the particular universe as an ethnographer formulates them. It is by noting how these laws vary from one universe to another and under what conditions, that the comparativist arrives at a statement of laws governing the separate sets of laws which in turn govern the events in their respective social universes.[24]

ABOUT CAUSES OF CULTURE STRESS

I have proposed a test of culture stress theory by a cross-cultural survey in which correlations are measured between hypothesized symptoms of culture stress and hypothesized causes. This report concerns itself chiefly with symptoms, because the selection of some plausible causes is easy. A wide range of causes of culture stress has been suggested by Honigmann.[25] These include failure of the culture to satisfy biological and psychological needs, presence of unrealizable social goals, presence of socially patterned terrors, frequency of catastrophic social events, and presence of contradictory social demands. Arsenian and Arsenian [26] list seven plausible causes of culture stress, all concerned with the nature of cultural goals—most important of these in their opinion is the proportion of the population having access to cultural goals.

The only question is whether existing ethnological reports have enough reliable information on hypothesized causes for a good cross-cultural survey. I submit that there are at least four aspects of culture in its relationship to environment which are known to vary widely, which may plausibly be hypothesized as causes of variation in culture stress, and on which there are now known to be abundant data in existing ethnological literature. Each of these hypothetical causes of culture stress has been the subject of at least one detailed and lengthy treatise and each is by its nature readily observable by field workers or elicitable from informants.

1. Ecological Pressure

Culture is first of all a system of extracting from a given environment a set of needed material things—in part the needs are biologically fixed, and in part they themselves are culturally determined. In some cultures there is a sufficiency of material needs, as defined by the culture (noting that sufficient food and shelter for health are everywhere recognized as universal human needs). In other cultures there is not enough to go around. In some cultures many culture bearers die of hunger; in other cultures death from hunger is unknown. Cultural ecology has long interested anthropologists and geographers; there are ample data on this topic.[27]

2. Economic Pressure

Some cultures provide regular systems for distributing material needs to all their members; other set up systems of competition, in which there is a realistic threat of deprivation of the needs of some people because others are encouraged by the culture to accumulate as much as possible—perhaps even to waste it conspicuously. There are ample data on economic systems among primitive people.[28]

3. Warfare

Some cultures (more accurately, some culture areas) display patterns of intense warfare with frequent loss of life and destruction of property. Other cultures characteristically settle intergroup conflicts with ceremonial combats involving little loss of life or property (a pattern especially common among the more primitive cultures). There are abundant data on primitive warfare.[29]

4. Sexual Deprivation

Some cultures impose severe limits on the achievement of sexual satisfaction by one or both sexes—for example, in some societies most available women become wives of older, more wealthy or influential men with the result that many men past puberty have restricted sexual access to women, and in some societies either or both sexes are expected to remain continent for several years (sometimes a decade or more) after puberty. Other cultures impose no such limits; instead a person of either sex from puberty on is likely to find a licit sexual partner readily available. There are abundant data on sexual regulations among primitive people.[30]

ABOUT SYMPTOMS OF CULTURE STRESS

Thus in designing a rigorous test of the culture stress theory, there is no difficulty in assembling a varied array of culture traits which seem plausible causes of culture stress and about which there are abundant useful data in existing ethnological reports. But when we turn from causes to symptoms of culture stress, we run into trouble. The present work reports the results of a search for such symptoms. A sample of 45 peoples was examined, and usable data found on these 37: *North America:* Ojibwa, Iroquois, Navaho, Harney Valley Paiute, Southeast Salish, Aleut, Copper Eskimo, Omaha; *South America:* Timbira, Barama River Carib, Jivaro, Tupinamba, Cuna, Siriono; *Africa:* Tanala, Azande, Ashanti, Mbundu, Chagga, Thonga, Tiv; *Asia:* Korea, Miao, Cambodians, Laotians, Vietnamese, Todas, Rwala, Hainanese, Khasi; *Oceania:* Tikopia, Pukapuka, Central Bisayans, Ifugao, Apayao, Ifalik, Aranda. The data were chiefly taken from the Human Relations Area Files at the University of Southern California, supplemented by some conventional library sources. The Human Relations Area Files are an especially convenient assemblage of ethnological field reports, in which the material is coded and filed by topic.[31] Sets of these files are available for checking at the following Universities: Chicago, Colorado, Cornell, Harvard, Hawaii, Indiana, Iowa, Michigan, North Carolina, Oklahoma, Paris (École pratique des hautes études), Pennsylvania, Princeton, Southern California, Southern Illinois, Utah, Washington, and Yale.

Data on four categories proved rich enough for use: (1) suicide (useful data on 21 societies), (2) homicide (useful data on 17 societies), (3) alcoholism (useful data on 25 societies), and (4) witchcraft (useful data on 31 societies). These are discussed further below. Five other categories proved disappointing: there were not enough data in the files on (1) *use of narcotics,* (2) *personality disorders,* (3) *offenses against the mores other than homicide,* (4) *psychosomatic illnesses,* or (5) *stuttering.* Concerning psychosomatic illnesses, data were particularly sought on eight complaints: (1) infertility, (2) rheumatism, (3) gastritis, (4) ulcers, (5) goiter, (6) diabetes, (7) cardiovascular hypertensions, and (8) neurodermatitis. Of these, infertility proved to be the only complaint mentioned at all often, and even on it no clinical details were ever given. The rarity of mention in ethnological reports of any of these complaints may conceivably be significant, since there is much mention of such communicable diseases as yaws, smallpox, and measles.

A Note on Stuttering

It is too bad that there is so little data on stuttering. It would seem to be a particularly promising cross-cultural indicator of culture stress.[32] Among modern Euro-American societies, the prevalence of stuttering among school children is variously reported as between about 8 and 30 per 1,000.[33] Apparently, comparably high rates occur among many Indian tribes of the Northwest Coast culture area.[34] However, there is good reason to believe that the rate is well below this among the Bannock and Shoshone of southeastern Idaho, where Snidecor, a speech therapist, interviewed over 800 Indians and failed to find one pure-blooded Indian who stuttered.[35] Kluckhohn found only three stutterers among 492 Ramah Navaho.[36] Elizabeth Q. White, a native Hopi who taught school on the Hopi reservation for nearly 20 years and in that time had well over 800 Hopi pupils, can recall only one stutterer—that child was the son of a Hopi mother and a Mexican father, born off the reservation.[37] Many ethnologists queried after their return from the field could recall no stutterers among the natives they studied; [38] however, there is considerable doubt that this kind of report means much: ethnologists must spend many years living among a given group before they themselves become good informants on a question like the prevalence of stuttering.

While there is wide disagreement among psychologists, psychiatrists, and speech therapists [39] about causes of stuttering, many hold that it is often a symptom of emotional stress, a reaction to situational factors. Cross-cultural field studies of stuttering could provide decisive tests of conflicting theories of its causes.

Unfortunately, existing literature on stuttering among primitive societies is completely inadequate today. Among all the reports in the Human Relations Area Files studied, not one gave deliberate attention to stuttering; through incidental allusions in some other connection, it appears that stuttering does occur among at least five societies in this sample: the Navaho, the Ojibwa, the Iroquois, the Azande, and the Miao.

CHAPTER 3

A Tentative Index of Culture Stress

Fortunately, much useful data did turn up on four hypothesized symptoms of culture stress: suicide, homicide, use of alcohol, and sorcery. From these I propose four indicators of culture stress: protest suicide, defiant homicide, drunken brawling, and witchcraft attribution. If the test of culture stress theory we have been talking about turns out well, then these four indicators can be combined into a crude index of culture stress. Until then, the tentative index has no scientific base but is only an untested proposal which seems interesting to many people. The study reported in this book is not a study of the validity of the index but only a data quality control study of the reliability of its indicators. In order to reduce the need for comparativist's inferences to a minimum, special pains are taken to define each trait precisely.

David Hays has suggested in conversation that these four indicators may be measures of two basic variables: overt aggression and covert aggression. The drunken brawling and defiant homicide indicators may present two successive levels of overt aggression, while the protest suicide and witchcraft attribution indicators may present two successive levels of covert aggression. Let us consider each of the proposed indicators in detail: (1) theory and previous research supporting the proposition that the indicator reflects culture stress, (2) a formal set of definitions, rules, and corollaries delimiting the indicator, (3) the range of functional variation of the indicator in varying cultural contexts, and (4) the problem of validating the indicator.

THE DRUNKEN BRAWLING INDICATOR

In recent years there has been lively interest in the role of cultural differences in alcoholism, that is, in pathological alcoholic addiction. The extensive literature, which documents the wide variation in prevalence of alcoholism from subculture to subculture in our own society as well as from culture to culture in other societies both civilized and primitive, is reviewed in Lemert[1] and Snyder.[2] However, as Lemert points out,[3] there is an unfortunate tendency in this literature to assume that all inebriation is "an expression of deprivation in personality or of defective social organization."

Drunken Brawling as a Symptom of Culture Stress

I assume only that alcohol often releases feelings of aggression otherwise inhibited, an assumption strongly supported by the cross-cultural survey of alcohol use in primitive societies by Horton.[4] Horton sees several prime functions in the use of alcohol by the peoples in his sample: reduction of feelings of anxiety,[5] release of aggressive impulses,[6] and release of sexual impulses.[7] Horton's study reports much data supporting these views, and more data in support is produced by Bales.[8]

The drunken brawling indicator here proposed distinguishes among alcohol-using societies between those with overt, easily recognizable symptoms of aggressive feelings released when people are in their cups and those where such clear evidence of aggressive feelings is lacking. (Data on pathological alcoholic addiction as distinguished from mere use of alcohol is very rare in existing ethnological literature.) No assumption is made that the mere use of alcohol is necessarily maladaptive or undesirable or itself a symptom of culture stress. It is my personal view that among many societies including our own (and its American Anthropological Association) alcohol plays a useful role in ceremonial drinking.

It seems proper to distinguish drunken brawls from sober brawls because the latter may well have judicial or political functions—hence they seem less plausibly a symptom of sheer anxiety or displaced hostility. And as a matter of fact it is unusual to have data on brawling but lack data on drinking of alcoholic beverages, so not much information is thrown away by this theoretically preferable indicator.

Definitions, Rules, and Corollaries

Definition 1.0 Drunken Brawling. The regular occurrence of physical assault among members of a single community while intoxicated.

Definition 1.1. Regular Occurrence. Where invariably drunken brawling occurs in most communities at least once a year.

Definition 1.2. Community. The local group, neighborhood or settlement. Where people do not gather in bands or live in villages or towns, the local ceremonial group.

Definition 1.3. Intoxicated. Any person who drinks any alcoholic beverage at all is presumed to be intoxicated from that time until he next goes to sleep.

Rule 1.4. No Intoxicants. Where the people do not use

intoxicating drinks at all, this is treated as a case of no data rather than as a case of no brawling.

Corollary 1.5. Physical Assault. Blows, wrestling, biting, hair-pulling, scratching and the like but not mere angry words, however offensive, or gestures, however threatening.

Range of Functional Variation

As it happens, the wide and varying use of alcohol in our own society (solitary drinking, family mealtime drinking, cocktail parties, sacerdotal drinking in both Christian and Jewish ritual) with its elaboration into such patterns as the French mode of selecting and evaluating table wines, makes the general range of alcohol use familiar to all readers. Cross-culturally, there are of course wide differences in emphasis, but I know of no use of alcohol in any other society not paralleled by an analogous one in our own.

Validation Problem

Since nothing is said about community size, it could be argued that frequency of drunken brawling is a simple function of mere size of community population. This argument is perfectly plausible a priori, but it is tested below by the data from this sample and discredited: there is no statistically significant relationship either between brawling and population of largest settlement ($Q = 0.37$) or, even more importantly, between brawling and total population ($Q = -\ 0.02$). While I have seen nothing to encourage the belief that innate physiological differences or purely physiological pathology are factors affecting the frequency of drunken brawling, I am not prepared to deny that possibility. A much more important limitation on the value of drunken brawling as an indicator of culture stress is that two other cultural factors must also be considered: the attitudes of the culture toward drinking and brawling, and the other alternate avenues of expression of culture stress which the culture affords.[9] So it does not necessarily follow from the fact that drunken brawling is common among the Tupinamba but unknown among the Toda that the Toda way of life is less stressful than the Tupinamba way of life. In this as in the other indicators, we seek no more than a measure which will distinguish the mean level of culture stress among two statistical arrays—here one array with drunken brawling frequent and the other an array with drunken brawling rare or unknown.

THE DEFIANT HOMICIDE INDICATOR

In contrast to the richness of theoretical work on suicide, little of value has been done on the causes of homicide.

Homicide as a Symptom of Culture Stress

In his survey of homicide in the United States, Brearly [10] cites many cultural factors as suspected explanations for high rates of homicide. But the only formal test of a cultural causation hypothesis known to me is the study of suicide and homicide by Henry and Short.[11] These men find that homicide rates in the United States in recent decades have varied in many circumstances inversely with suicide rates. While suicide rates rise in depression and fall in prosperity, crimes of violence rise in prosperity and fall in depression. While suicide rates correlate positively with social status, homicide rates correlate negatively; but while suicide rates correlate negatively with strength of social ties, homicide rates correlate positively. Henry and Short explain homicide, like suicide, as a manifestation of feelings of aggression and attribute feelings of aggression to experiences of frustration. Thus the Henry and Short study provides support for the hypothesis that homicide often occurs as a response to culture stress.

Definitions, Rules, and Corollaries

Definition 2.0. Defiant Homicide. Deliberate homicides committed in such a way as to come to public notice despite disapproval not only by a majority of the kin of the slayer but also by a majority of the members of the ethnic group studied.

Definition 2.1. Kin. The grandparents of the slayer and their descendants.

Rule 2.2. Clandestine Homicide, in which the slayer conceals his participation though not the fact of homicide, is presumed to be disapproved by a majority of ethnic group members in the absence of evidence to the contrary.

Rule 2.3. Blood Revenge is presumed to be approved by a majority of the kin of the slayer in the absence of evidence to the contrary. Otherwise, disapproval of homicide by the kin of the slayer is presumed in the absence of evidence to the contrary.

Corollary 2.4. Accidental homicides are not defiant homicides, even though the culture pattern in question may class them as murder or manslaughter.

Corollary 2.5. Publicly approved homicides are not defiant homicides. Examples of publicly approved homicides: (A) executions as punishment for actual or alleged offenses against the mores, where both the punishment and the manner of execution are publicly approved or condoned whether formally (as in a state execution) or informally (as in a lynching); (B) ceremonial sacrifices, whether for religious purposes (for instance, at an Aztec temple) or for secular purposes (for instance, at a Tlingit potlatch); (C) killing the enemy in warfare.

Corollary 2.6. Homicides committed in the regular course of business by members of professional castes or bands of thieves or brigands or assassins are not defiant homicides provided the values of the caste or band subculture are accepted or condoned by a majority of the kin of the members (for example, the peasant brigands of nineteenth-century Lucania [12]).

Corollary 2.7. Homicides committed to avenge personal offenses (other homicides, adultery, insults) are not defiant homicides provided the act is approved or condoned either by the public or by a majority of the kin of the slayer.

Corollary 2.8. Homicides disguised by the slayer as suicides or accidental deaths are not defiant homicides.

Range of Functional Variation

As the foregoing corollaries indicate, there seems to be an even wider cross-cultural range of functional variation among homicides than among suicides. And often the determination of the true reasons in the mind of the slayer for a given homicide must be even more difficult than the determination of the reasons for a given suicide. However, it is obviously not difficult to distinguish those homicides where the slayer and his kin claim a publicly approved context from those where they do not make such a claim. I offer as a working hypothesis, then, that defiant homicide is commonly an indicator of cultural stress on the slayer, stress driving him to defy public opinion so seriously.

Validation Problem

In this as in the other indicators, we seek no more than a measure that will distinguish the mean level of culture stress among two statistical arrays—here one array with defiant homicide level high, the other with defiant homicide level low. It is clear that, like drunken brawling, defiant homicide reflects not only cultural stress but also other factors. I am not prepared to deny that defiant homicide sometimes is committed by the mentally ill, nor to deny that mental illness sometimes results from physiological rather than cultural factors. Here again, defiant homicide, like drunken brawling, reflects to some extent the availability of alternate responses to culture stress provided by the culture pattern; some of these alternate responses are reflected in other indicators of this index, but other alternate responses are not. So here again it does not necessarily follow from the fact that there is a higher rate of defiant homicide among the Tupinamba than among the Tanala that the Tupinamba way of life is more stressful than the Tanala way of life.

THE PROTEST SUICIDE INDICATOR

Suicide is a problem that has fascinated psychiatrists, sociologists, and psychoanalysts alike—all the approaches to the study of mental health have considered suicide a fruitful topic of investigation. It is beyond the scope of this monograph to review in detail the extensive theoretical literature on suicide; full treatment would require a lengthy treatise in intellectual history, but there are excellent recent summaries by Schneider [13] and Jackson.[14] I mention here only theories which attribute an important role to some kind of culture stress. There is no doubt that this is but a partial and incomplete element in understanding suicide. Durkheim's work, for example, for all its unquestionable value, fails to shed any light on the reasons why one white Protestant male middle-aged married Los Angeles bookkeeper commits suicide while another does not. To understand fully any specific case of suicide, personality factors, subconscious mechanisms, and psychotic difficulties—perhaps even organic pathology in some cases—may be essential. Yet, as even so hard a critic of Durkheim as Schneider [15] concedes, his data shows that sociocultural differences certainly affect suicide rates. It is sociocultural differences which interest us here. I readily concede that to clinicians interested in a theory of suicide which will help them diagnose potential suicides in advance this point of view has little to offer. But we are here interested in suicide, not as a clue to individual difficulties (although it certainly is that), but only as a clue to cultural stress.

There was considerable dispute in the older literature about the incidence of suicide among peoples at different levels of social and cultural evolution.[16] Some argued that suicide was rarer among primitive people than civilized, others that it was more frequent. The research here reported tends to support the view that both these positions may be misleading, that in fact there may be a greater *variance* in suicide rates among primitive societies than among civilized societies. Even after allowing for extrapolation error from small samples (a topic discussed in detail later), one of the societies in the sample here considered has a much higher suicide rate than any reliably reported in the 1956 *United Nations Demographic Yearbook* (that is, substantially complete returns with a maximum of 10 per cent of all deaths attributed to the category of senility or unknown causes).[17] Others appear to have much lower rates.

Suicide as a Symptom of Culture Stress

In his classic study of suicide, Durkheim,[18] writing at the close of the nineteenth century found correlations in data from Western European countries between suicide rates and such sociocultural factors as religion, occupation, military rank, marital status, and economic cycle. To explain these correlations, Durkheim distinguished three basic social types of suicide: egoistic, altruistic, and anomic. In Durkheim's view, egoistic suicide results from a relaxation of the bonds tying man to society, altruistic suicide is committed for the benefit of society in support of some social value, and anomic suicide results from a sudden change in the social situation which imposes upon the actor the necessity for a large-scale readjustment. Durkheim's pupil Halbwachs [19] corrected many of Durkheim's errors of method and amplified his data, reporting correlations between suicide rates and size of cities, direction of population flow, marital status, and religion. Neither Durkheim nor Halbwachs used the calculus of probabilities; they did not compute coefficients of correlation or association, test the significance of differences or in any way deal with the null hypothesis that their observed results merely reflect chance or random differences. Despite this shortcoming, their work provides impressive support for the view that cultural stress is an important factor in suicide.

By far the most sophisticated test of a culture stress theory of suicide is the previously mentioned study of Henry and Short.[20] They report that in the United States in recent decades suicide rates have fallen in prosperous years and risen in depression years. They see both suicide and homicide as expressions of aggression. Feelings of aggression, they hypothesize, often result from experiences of frustration. Business cycles in the United States produce variations in the hierarchical ranking of persons and consequently produce frustrations among people oriented toward maintaining or raising their hierarchical position. Their interpretation of their data agrees with Durkheim that there is an inverse relationship between the strength of social ties and the suicide rate. Since suicide rates correlate positively with social status and negatively with strength of social ties, Henry and Short conclude that in general suicide varies negatively with the strength of external restraints over behavior. Thus they provide further support for the view that culture stress is an important factor in suicide.

Definitions, Rules, and Corollaries

Definition 3.0. Protest Suicide. Voluntary suicide committed in such a way as to come to public notice.

Definition 3.1. Involuntary Suicide. Suicide committed to avoid capital punishment or as part of a customary rite where the suicide is designated by custom or by another person.

Definition 3.2. Voluntary Suicide. Suicide committed in any other circumstances.

Definition 3.3. Suicide. The conscious, deliberate killing by a person of himself.

Corollary 3.4. A person who kills himself in response to an unconscious death wish, a person who in effect proves fatal-accident prone, has not committed protest suicide.

Corollary 3.5. A person who deliberately kills himself (or fails to save himself from threatened death when he could have done so) but does so in such a way that other people may readily mistake the event for an involuntary death has not committed protest suicide.

Range of Functional Variation

Suicide has a wide range of functional settings. There are variations in cultural approval, from situations like those in Japan, where suicide is often seen as the proper, dignified, admirable course to be carried out in a formal ceremony, to those in German-speaking countries, where suicide is formally denounced as immoral and illegal but informally considered an honorable—sometimes the only honorable— course of action, to those in medieval England, where suicide was felt to be an unnatural and abhorrent act, an act hardly to be thought of by a person of sound mind. There are variations in occasion: the aged Eskimo who suicides in order not to be a burden to his family in its difficult struggle for food, the Miao volunteer who suicides in an annual religious ceremony for the benefit of his fellow tribesmen, the American business failure who suicides to avoid a sudden drop in social status, the Fijian girl who suicides to avoid marrying a man she does not like, the Iroquois wife who suicides because her husband is unfaithful to her, the Paiute mother who suicides because her child has died, and so on. Wisse [21] distinguishes nine major categories of reported causes of suicide among primitive peoples: (1) material causes: age, illness, bodily pains, beatings, poverty, hunger; (2) grave escort; (3) grief at death of a loved one; (4) religious suicide, associated with a belief in immortality, or out of fear of spirits or to propitiate the gods; (5) resentment or despondency at captivity or removal from native country; (6) sexual frustration, either because of rejection by or loss of a love partner, because of forced marriage, or because of jealousy at the unfaithfulness of a spouse or lover; (7) hypertrophy of a sense of personal dignity: shame, injured pride, sense of honor, guilt; (8) sudden impulse when emotionally upset through anger, domestic quarrels, censure, "weariness of life from causes of little cogency, trivialities"; and (9) revenge.

How reliable are reports of causes of this kind? By what kind of inquiry do ethnographers determine the circumstances surrounding a suicide? Speaking of European statistical returns, Durkheim points out:

But as Wagner long ago remarked, what are called statistics of the motives of suicide are actually statistics of the opinions concerning such motives of officials, often of lower officials, in charge of this information service. Unfortunately, official establishments of fact are known to be often defective even when applied to obvious material facts comprehensible to any conscientious observer and leaving no room for evaluation. How suspect must they be considered when applied not simply to recording an accomplished fact but to its interpretation and explanation? To determine the cause of a phenomenon is always a difficult problem. The scholar requires all sorts of observations and experiments to solve even one question. Now, human volition is the most complex of all phenomena. The value of improvised judgments, attempting to assign a definite origin for each special case from a few hastily collected bits of information is, therefore, obviously slight. As soon as some of the facts commonly supposed to lead to despair are thought to have been discovered in the victim's past, further search is considered useless, and his drunkenness or domestic unhappiness or business troubles are blamed, depending on whether he is supposed recently to have lost money, had home troubles or indulged in a taste for liquor.[22]

The European official whom Durkheim criticizes at least has the advantage of making his inquiries immediately after the event, when matters are still fresh in people's minds. Much of our ethnological data is collected about suicides occurring years or in some cases even generations earlier. While the simple fact that a person well known to the informant committed suicide can plausibly be supposed to remain in his memory, the details surrounding the event are another matter. Furthermore, it is extremely unusual for ethnographers to report case data on suicides in any detail. Consequently, let us adopt a procedure which makes us independent of judgments about cultural context of protest suicide. Let us take as our working hypothesis that usually a person who chooses protest suicide finds life hard or unpleasant in some way. Since his life is so largely a product of his culture—its opportunities, its demands, the satisfactions it affords and the burdens it imposes—we take a voluntary protest suicide to indicate culture stress whatever the surrounding circumstances or cultural attitudes toward suicide. The validity of this working hypothesis is our next topic.

Validation Problem

This working hypothesis must of course remain tentative and provisional until successfully tested. The test of the theory of culture stress we have proposed would, if successful and otherwise satisfactory, provide impressive support for the hypothesis that many instances of protest suicide reflect cultural stress.

True, here again, as with drunken brawling and defiant homicide, this working hypothesis drastically oversimplifies matters. In the first place, I am not prepared to deny that suicide sometimes results from mental illness, and I am not prepared to deny that mental illness in turn sometimes results from physiological rather than cultural factors.

In the second place, it must be supposed that variations in protest suicide rate reflect not only individual mental health and individual response to culture stress but also reflect cultural attitudes toward suicide. Perhaps it could be argued that culture patterns permit or encourage suicide when such a release from tension is needed because of the stresses imposed. But this is a problem for research. And, unfortunately, many of our ethnographical reports are silent on the attitude of the people toward suicide.

In the third place, the protest suicide rate reflects to some extent the availability of alternate responses to culture stress provided by the culture pattern. Some of these alternate responses are reflected in other indicators, but others certainly are not.

So it does not necessarily follow from the fact that there is a higher rate of protest suicide among the Tupinamba than among the Tanala that the Tupinamba way of life is more stressful than the Tanala way of life. The working hypothesis here adopted is simply that of two statistical arrays differing in rate of protest suicide, the mean level of culture stress is higher in the array with the higher suicide rate. If in fact there turn out to be significant correlations between protest suicide rate and each of the hypothesized causes of culture stress and if in fact these correlations cannot be plausibly explained by sampling bias, historical association, informants' bias, or ethnographers' errors, then this working hypothesis is validated, at least provisionally. And all scientific generalizations are provisional.

THE WITCHCRAFT ATTRIBUTION INDICATOR

A number of anthropologists in recent years have suggested a connection between prevalence of belief in witchcraft and the general level of anxiety in a culture, a topic surveyed by Honigmann.[23] Hallowell [24] and Beatrice Whiting [25] emphasize the importance of loose social controls in calling forth the threat of witchcraft attribution as a social sanction. In her monograph on Paiute sorcery, Beatrice Whiting [26] sees witchcraft attribution primarily as a mechanism for the control of aggression. Aggressive feelings are clearly very high among these Indians; their suicide rate is extremely high and this Whiting explains as a manifestation of aggression.[27] She tests this theory in a cross-cultural survey of 50 tribes, reporting a negative correlation between the importance of sorcery on one hand and presence of an effective system of authoritative regulation of aggression through public officials on the other.[28]

Witchcraft Attribution as a Symptom of Culture Stress

While anthropologists like Hallowell and Beatrice Whiting have been chiefly interested in witchcraft attribution as a form of social pressure, a *cause* of cultural stress, other anthropologists have called attention to its function as a *symptom* of culture stress originating elsewhere. Honigmann [29] explains the high frequency of witchcraft attribution among many peoples like the Mbundu and the Kaska as a result of latent hostility, there being strong pressure upon Mbundu to suppress all manifestations or even feelings of hostility. Monica Wilson [30] attributes witch-fear among the Nyakyusa to anxiety about unequal wealth distribution, and that among the Pondo to anxiety about limited sexual opportunities. These findings are supported by a comparative study of four other African societies by Nadel,[31] who reported witchcraft "causally as well as conspicuously related to specific anxieties and stresses arising in social life." [32] These views are likewise generally supported by the cross-cultural survey of Whiting and Child already discussed: they correlated "fear of other human beings" (that is, illness explained as the result of witchcraft [33]) with over-all socialization anxiety and reported significant positive correlation.[34]

In some ways the most impressive support of all for the hypothesis that witchcraft attribution reflects cultural stress comes from the study of Navaho witchcraft by Kluckhohn,[35] a report of outstanding quality. Kluckhohn [36] reviews a considerable number of adaptive functions of belief in witchcraft among the Navaho. While not all of these seem related to cultural stress, the two chief ones seem clearly symptomatic of it. The symptomatic functions posited by Kluckhohn include: (1) release of aggressive feelings, either by displacement aggression through attribution of witchcraft to distant Navaho against whom no retaliation is intended [37] or by direct aggression through accusation of witchcraft leveled at a local community member with the intention of injuring him through gossip and other sanctions [38] and (2) lowering of the general level of anxiety feelings among the

Navaho,[39] feelings which he attributes largely to the socialization patterns of Navaho society.[40] These two symptomatic functions are in Kluckhohn's opinion the most important latent functions of witchcraft in Navaho culture.[41]

Definitions, Rules, and Corollaries

Definition 4.0. Frequent Witchcraft Attribution. Witchcraft attribution is frequent where a majority of the deaths thought due to supernatural causes are attributed to witchcraft rather than to the acts of gods or spirits alone.

Definition 4.1. Supernatural Causes. Prerequisite events occurring outside the body of the dead person and not identifiable by reliable sensory evidence.

Definition 4.2. Witchcraft. Supernatural causes intentionally produced by the acts of living people.

Rule 4.3. No Supernatural Explanations of Death. Where none of the people ever attribute death to supernatural causes, this is treated as a case of no data rather than as a case of no witchcraft attribution.

Corollary 4.4. Human Influence on Spirits. Where a death is attributed to the act of a spirit procured for the purpose by a living person, this constitutes witchcraft attribution.

Rule 4.5. Inconsistent Theories. Where more than one mutually incompatible theory about the causes of death is held, the theory attributing the largest importance to witchcraft is taken as the basis for the witchcraft attribution indicator.

Range of Functional Variation

In most societies witchcraft is disapproved and witchcraft attribution alleges a serious moral delinquency, but there are societies in which its use is condoned or even approved. There is wide variation in the identity of alleged sorcerers:

in some societies they are foreigners, in other societies in-group members of high status, in others close relatives of the alleged victim, and in still others, any of these. The motives people ascribe to sorcerers, that allegedly lead them to practice witchcraft, likewise vary widely from culture to culture: revenge, economic gain, and political power are among the causes most frequently mentioned. Among many societies where witchcraft is important, knowledge of the topic is likely to be construed as evidence that the informant is himself a witch; consequently, accurate and detailed data of the ideas of the people may be very hard to come by. I offer as a researchable working hypothesis that whatever the circumstances, by producing feelings of anger, hostility or anxiety, cultural stress is an important factor in stimulating witchcraft attribution.

Validation Problem

Witchcraft attribution often has other functions than to give relief from distressing feelings of anxiety or aggression and there are other ways than witchcraft attribution of relieving such feelings. So once again it does not necessarily follow from the fact that witchcraft attribution is common among the Tupinamba but rare among the Tanala that the Tupinamba way of life is more stressful than the Tanala way of life. Once again I say that in this as in the other indicators, we seek no more than a measure which will distinguish the mean level of culture stress among two statistical arrays— here one array with witchcraft attribution frequent, the other an array with witchcraft attribution infrequent.

INDEX CONSTRUCTION

Table 1 shows the application of all four indicators to construct an index of culture stress. The index is calculated

Table 1—Index of Culture Stress

People	Drunken Brawling	Defiant Homicide	Protest Suicide	Witchcraft Attribution	C.S. Index
Ifalik	L	—	L	L	0.0
Toda	L	L	L	L	0.0
Cambodia	L	—	L	L	0.0
Tanala	—	L	L	L	0.0
Copper Eskimo	—	H	L	L	0.33
Cuna (San Blas)	H	L	—	L	0.33
Iroquois	H	L	L [a]	—	0.33
Apayao	H	—	L	L	0.33
Siriono	H	L	—	L	0.33
Aleut	H	L	H	L	0.50
Vietnam	H	—	H [b]	L	0.66
Jivaro	L	—	H	H	0.66
Miao	—	L	H	H	0.66
Ojibwa	H	L	—	H	0.66
Azande	H	—	L	H	0.66
S.E. Salish (Sanpoil)	H	H	H	L	0.75
Navaho	H	H	L [c]	H	0.75
Northern Paiute (Harney Valley)	H	H	H	H	1.0
Tupinamba	H	H	H	H	1.0
Timbira (Ramkokamekra)	—	L	—	—	—
Ashanti	L	—	—	L	—
Laos	—	L	—	—	—
Hainan	L	—	—	—	—
Omaha	H	—	—	L	—
Chagga	H	—	—	L	—
Korea	—	—	H	L	—
Khasi	—	H	—	L	—
Rwala	—	—	H	L	—
Ifugao	L	—	—	H	—
Tikopia	—	—	H	L	—
Pukapuka	—	—	H	L	—
Central Bisayans	H	—	—	—	—
Aranda	—	—	—	H	—
Thonga	—	—	—	H	—
Tiv	—	H	—	H	—
Carib (Barama River)	H	—	—	H	—
Mbundu	—	—	H	H	—

a. Seneca only.   b. Hanoi only.   c. San Juan County only.

KEY: L = Low
     H = High
     — = No Data

only for ethnic units about which there are data on at least three of the four indicators. The index consists of the ratio of the number of "high" indicators to the total number of indicators on which there is data. Ideally, an index number should be derived from a large number of indicators which have low correlations with each other but high correlations with the phenomenon being measured. Each indicator should represent a part of the total phenomenon measured by the index, and be weighted to reflect the importance of its part.[42]

The present sample suggests low positive correlations between the four indicators. Yule's Q coefficient of association [43] was computed to indicate the relationship between the values in this sample with the results given in Table 2.

Table 2

	Defiant Homicide	Drunken Brawling	Witchcraft Attribution
Protest suicide	0.38	0.50	0.30
Defiant homicide	—	0.23	0.66
Drunken brawling	—	—	0.35

None of these associations are significant at the 5 per cent level, using as a test of significance Fisher's exact test [44] as tabled by Mainland et al.[45] This is a nonparametric test of randomness of allocation which assumes *only* independence of cases—nothing more. (However, a significant result in the present application might of course reflect sampling bias or historical association rather than the functional association arising out of culture stress which interests us here.)

Four indicators of culture stress are certainly a modest number, but, as reported above, I could find no other plausible symptoms of culture stress on which enough data were available in existing ethnographic reports. Some other possibilities have since been suggested by colleagues in conversation: wife beating might be a symptom of culture stress among men (Nora Weckler); beating, kicking or tormenting of dogs might conceivably also be a stress symptom (Charles Mudd); contact with Western culture might well be a cause of culture stress and hence rise in frequency or intensity of a factor after contact with Euro-American culture might tend to support the hypothesis that the factor is a stress symptom (Nora Weckler). The study of reactions to bereavement by Volkart and Michael [46] suggest that here may be still another useful indicator.

In the absence of any plausible grounds for weighting some symptoms more heavily than others, all four symptoms are weighted equally—an arbitrary assumption. Offhand, it seems entirely unlikely that all four are in fact equivalent measures. On the contrary, the indicators seem to show a tendency toward forming Guttman scales. No case in this sample occurs in which defiant homicide (DH) is high when drunken brawling (DB) is low; and there are only two cases in which protest suicide is low while witchcraft attribution is high.

Validation Problem

We have already reviewed the theories and previous research which support the plausibility that each of these indicators reflects culture stress in some way. As we have seen, all four indicators seem plausibly a reflection of feelings of aggression, which in turn are thought by many psychologists often to result from frustration; furthermore, all four indicators have been linked by some theorists with feelings of anxiety.

However, it seems clear that each of these indicators *also* reflects the cultural attitude toward that kind of behavior.

In one culture with a high level of aggression and/or anxiety, suicide (or homicide or witchcraft attribution) may be inhibited because the culture disapproves expression of these feelings, while in another culture with a lower level of aggression and/or anxiety, cultural inhibitions may be absent.

Three of the four indicators (all except protest suicide) operate to some extent to provide release from tensions and thus to a certain extent themselves lower the over-all culture stress level of the people. However, as Herbert Kelman points out in a letter to me, "witchcraft attribution may be an adaptive way of reducing the over-all amount of anxiety, but it is still an indication of the fact that there is a lot of anxiety which needs to be reduced." The same of course can be said for drunken brawling—and perhaps conceivably also for defiant homicide.

The indicators reflect not only the pressures upon the people from the cultural situation but also the training in the culture pattern to endure or support stress. Extreme examples of severe training—itself highly stressful—that has the effect of preparing people to endure later, more severe stresses are the recruit training programs of many military organizations—for example, the "boot camps" of the United States Marine Corps.

Finally, each of these indicator traits—and no doubt many other traits not considered here, as well—to a certain extent provide alternate ways of relieving feelings of aggression and/or anxiety or other feelings resulting from culture stress. I do not doubt that of two cultures with approximately equal levels of culture stress, one may have high suicide and low homicide while the other may have the reverse. This effect may explain the fact that several investigators have found negative correlations between suicide and homicide *within* the generally similar Euro-American culture area while this cross-cultural study has found a positive correlation (albeit a nonsignificant one).

To some extent, the calculation of a culture stress index, as in Table 1, overcomes the foregoing difficulties by "averaging out" the factors. However, it introduces a new and quite implausible assumption—that each of these indicators is equivalent to every other as a measure of culture stress. (Furthermore, in a few cases data from one indicator come from a different period in time or portion of the unit studied than data from another indicator). The fact that the Jivaro have a culture stress index of 0.66 while the Aleut have one of 0.50 does not necessarily mean that Jivaro culture is more highly stressful than Aleut culture. Even the fact that the Tupinamba have a culture stress index of 1.0 while the Toda have one of 0.0 may conceivably be misleading—though here the difference is so great as to create in my mind at least a substantial presumption that the general level of culture stress is higher among the Tupinamba than the Toda.

However, the culture stress index is designed to measure not individual peoples like the Toda or the Tupinamba, but statistical arrays of peoples in a cross-cultural survey sample. Here the warning of Goodenough already quoted is worth repeating: "what we do as ethnographers is and must be kept independent of what we do as comparative ethnologists." If our goal is to understand Tupinamba or Toda culture, the culture stress index will be of little use to us; there is no substitute for full study of Tupinamba or Toda culture in all its richness. Categories like "defiant homicide" or "protest suicide" have little place there; what we want instead are detailed studies of Toda or Tupinamba suicide and homicide.

The limitations of an index of the kind here proposed

resemble those of an intelligence test. While an intelligence test is a useful crude approximation for the study of the mind of a child, it is far inferior to a careful and detailed look at his school performance, his home situation, his interests and his emotional problems. Where the intelligence test comes into its own is as a tool for handling *groups* of children: through its use, school classes can be quickly and efficiently sorted by learning ability; and while no doubt this sorting will be far from error-free, a high proportion of the students so sorted will be put into the intended category.

Furthermore, just as an intelligence test tests only those skills which it tests (and many people feel that the best operating definition of "intelligence" is that capability which an intelligence test measures), so this index measures only those culture stress symptoms which it measures. The extent to which people who test low on intelligence tests display useful abilities of various sorts is a problem for research; the value of intelligence tests arises from the occurrence of high correlations between performance on such tests and other kinds of performance. The value of the index proposed here—if it has any value—will be shown by the test of culture stress theory proposed in Chapter 2. If there are correlations between hypothesized causes and these hypothesized symptoms, I submit this finding would show that the culture stress index is a useful tool in research.

The purpose for which this index is intended is the statistical test of hypotheses in cross-cultural surveys. I seek no more than a measure that will distinguish the mean level of culture stress between two statistical arrays—one array with mean index score low, the other with mean index score high. If in the proposed test of culture stress theory the over-all index score has a higher correlation with hypothetical causes of culture stress than any of the individual indicators, its value will have been demonstrated; if not, its value will be indeed doubtful. In effect, then, the index is now merely a model of culture stress symptoms whose value in research remains doubtful until shown.[47]

CHAPTER 4

Controlling the Ethnological Research Process

The problem of the present study is the reliability of the four indicators of culture stress just described. Are the data in existing ethnological reports reliable enough to make possible a test of culture stress theory by a cross-cultural survey using the tentative index of culture stress proposed in Chapter 3? For example, how does an ethnographer really know what is the frequency of suicide or homicide? Are ethnological statistics of this sort worth anything at all? It is true that suicides and homicides which are disguised so as not to come to public notice as such are by definition excluded from our categories of protest suicide and defiant homicide. But even so, how reliable are field reports of suicide and homicide rates?

THE ETHNOLOGICAL RESEARCH PROCESS

Ethnographical reports are compiled in various ways and by people playing various roles in their intercourse with the people being studied. There are the natives themselves, who sometimes write ethnographic reports about themselves; such

77

authors usually are acculturated to European ways. There are professional anthropologists, who travel for the purpose of studying people and compiling reports on them. There are other kinds of scientists: explorers, like Lewis and Clark, whose chief interest is topography, or naturalists, like Wallace, whose chief interest is the nonhuman life of the lands they visit. There are missionaries, who seek to transmit Western culture in whole or in part to the peoples they live with. There are government officials, some political administrators, others soldiers or sailors, who seek to control the political behavior of the people they visit. Finally, there are European settlers, whether traders or farmers or trappers, who seek a livelihood in a new land, and thus introduce European economic culture.

Whatever the role played by the ethnographer among the people about whom he reports, he gets his information on their culture in one of three ways: by himself taking part in it, by passively but directly observing the life of the natives, or by questioning informants. (Information gathered by the historiographical method—the study of native writings—or by the archeological method—the study of the material remains of the culture of dead people—both are outside the scope of the present inquiry.)

Hypothetically, it would seem that participation in native culture would be the most powerful method of observation. However, it has a considerable number of limitations in practice. Unless he has been raised in the culture and is a native speaker of the language, a member of native kin groups by birth and also by marriage, and a sharer of native values, including native religion and native attitudes toward war and toward outsiders, the ethnographer can never fully participate in native culture; yet very few ethnographies have been written by natives meeting all these tests. But a native who acculturates to an alien, and in the nature of things, inevitably hostile culture does not any longer fully share his parental culture and indeed renounces some of its most central traits. A visiting ethnographer who tries to take part in native life may thus in many ways approximate the native experience, but few seriously go all the way to join the native culture by marrying natives and accepting for themselves the native kinship obligations, the native religion, laws, and mores, and the native political and military responsibilities. Thus, rarely does the author of an ethnographic report constitute himself a true and complete member of the society: rarely is he himself, then, a good informant. Participation in native life obviously is extremely valuable to an ethnographer—but only as a supplement to questioning informants, not as a substitute.

In the same way, the direct passive observation by an ethnographer of native life is extremely valuable as a supplement to the questioning of informants. But it often fails to be an adequate substitute. The ethnographer is usually concerned with the observation of culture patterns, repetitive programs of life. Unless he lives with the people a long time, he is not in a good position to decide whether a given event he watches is a typical sample of a repetitive pattern or not. In any case, he depends upon his informants to tell him the meaning of most events to the people.

So for most ethnographical data the informant remains the key man. The good informant is a full member of the society being studied—a native speaker, a "natural-born citizen." He is a respected member, in good standing with his fellows. He is a full participant in any subcultural complex for which he gives information—about women's affairs, the informant should be a woman; about the carpenters' guild, a member; and so on. He is intelligent, experienced, and interested in the work of recording his people's way of life. Very often it is the old men and women who make the ideal informants—they know the most, they like to talk, and they have lots of spare time.

The good ethnographer makes fast friends with several informants. He gains their confidence by performing friendly offices, by assuring them that all statements will be treated confidentially, and by being personally agreeable. In this way, day after day and week after week, in time he establishes the subtle and poorly understood personal connection which we call rapport, that electric feeling of mutual trust which characterizes interpersonal relations at their finest.

The good ethnographer trains his informant to report accurately and to distinguish what he himself has experienced from what he has only heard. The good ethnographer thoroughly masters the native language so that he needs use no interpreter or contact language. But if there is not time for this, he devotes care to the training of his interpreter so that the interpreter repeats the informants' statements as nearly as possible verbatim, paraphrasing as little as possible.

First-Stage Bias: The Informant's Mind

Since ethnographic reports depend so heavily upon native informants, control of informant bias is obviously an urgent task. We define an informant bias as a circumstance which leads informants consistently to form an erroneous mental image, or memory, of an event or culture pattern. (Where an informant has an accurate mental image but for reasons of his own makes a misleading report to an ethnographer, we class this as a second stage error, an ethnographer's error.) Three main sources of informant error occur. Perhaps the most common is the distorting influence of a cultural theory, or stereotype. A citizen of a large American city, for example, might report that its mayor is chosen by popular election: he is supposed to be, and in fact elections are regularly held as scheduled. A foreign ethnographer however might in some cities consider the elections mere ceremonial ratifications of the choice of a political boss. There are two well-known primitive societies, the Arunta and the Trobriands, where the people deny that there is a causal relationship between sexual intercourse and pregnancy; in both these societies, the cultural value system has another theory of pregnancy which is central to the people's ideology. So informants can form false mental images of patterns in their own culture because they are misled by their culture's theory of itself.

A second possible source of informant error might arise from a poor choice of informant by the ethnographer. Should the ethnographer question an informant about a subculture pattern with which the informant is not familiar, he might report his erroneous impressions of that activity. Men might not know much about childbirth in societies where only women are supposed to be present at the parturition scene.

A third possible source of informant error might arise from faulty memory of the details of a particular unique event. Historians, overwhelmingly concerned as a rule with the reconstruction of the details of unique events, are understandably skeptical of the accuracy of memoirs in which participants describe past events from memory. Should an informant have participated in only a single childbirth, either as principal or as attendant, she might well make such an error—about childbirth practices, for example. On the other hand, we submit that this kind of error is not likely to be made about repetitive patterns, events that take place over and over again according to a culturally dictated program.

Second-Stage Bias: The Ethnographer's Mind

Where an ethnographer personally witnesses an event or a practice, the first stage of observation is directly checked (but even then, often the ethnographer relies on the informant for assurance that the event witnessed is a typical example of a recurrent pattern). The major source of second stage error arises out of the dependence of ethnographers upon informants. Informants may lack candor: they may be unwilling either to answer a question truthfully or to decline to answer and may instead deliberately tell an untruth. There are many circumstances in which this is likely to happen. In some societies, people tend to give the answer they think the questioner wishes simply to please him— this is considered common courtesy. In our society, we are likely to do this, for example, when questioned by a woman about the attractiveness of her clothes.

Or often the informant may have, or may think he has, some benefit to be gained by misleading the foreign stranger. He may deny any belief in witchcraft when in fact he is terrified of sorcery because he does not want to seem knowledgeable on that subject, for fear of being thought a witch himself. He may conceal the size of his family, or its resources, from a census-taker because he thinks (perhaps correctly) that he will thus lower his burden of taxes or forced labor. He may simply be embarrassed to give a correct answer. In our society, questions about sex relations and personal income often produce intense embarrassment. In some societies, childbirth is considered a highly personal, private function, embarrassing to discuss with a stranger. Another common source of embarrassment may be self-consciousness about culture practices that the informant himself has begun to think of as "backward" or "primitive" because non-European. Since Europeans regularly give birth in a supine position, it is plausible to suppose that some informants might be tempted to mislead ethnographers by erroneously reporting the use of such a position among their people, simply in order to make them seem more "modern."

Another source of second-stage bias might be the theoretical orientation of a field worker, which might lead him to notice and report events and patterns which support a particular theory (Marxism, functionalism, capitalism, Freudianism) but to overlook and fail to report events and patterns that are inconsistent with such a theory.

Third-Stage Bias: The Comparativist's Mind

By the "comparativist" we mean the person doing the research, the individual reading the ethnographer's field reports and compiling statistics from them. Theoretically, a comparativist might deliberately falsify his reports. In many comparative studies, comparativists systematically cull evidence which favors their thesis and ignore evidence which favors the contrary thesis; this is the method used by forensic speakers and attorneys. Finally, a comparativist may tend to interpret vague or imprecise reports in a manner which favors the comparativist's thesis, like a baseball umpire who calls all the close ones in favor of the home team.

CONTROLLING FIRST-STAGE BIAS (INFORMANT'S MIND)

The present study offers controls for bias at each of the three stages of observation. These controls involve contrasting reports known to have been made under presumably better conditions of observation with those not so known. Wherever no information has come to hand about a given condition of observation, we have treated the report as made under the presumably poorer condition.

We have two quality control tests on informants' minds (see Table 3) and propose a third test for future use. All

Table 3—Data Quality Control Measurements

TEST NO.	OBSERVATION CONDITION MEASURED	Drunken Brawling	CULTURAL STRESS TRAIT Defiant Homicide	Protest Suicide	Witchcraft Attribution	STATISTICAL MEASURE USED
First-stage bias						
1.	Case reports	—	0.35	—0.89 [a]	—	Yule's Q
2.	Participant observation	0.38	0.00	0.078	0.50 [b]	Yule's Q
Second-stage bias						
3.	Length of stay	0.22	0.66	0.29	0.86 [c]	Yule's Q
4.	Native language familiarity	0.25	0.71	0.88	0.88	Yule's Q
5.	Ethnographer's role	—0.28	0.00	0.00	—0.57	Yule's Q
Third-stage bias						
6.	Explicitness and generality of reports	0.50	—0.80 [b]	—0.89 [d]	0.22	Yule's Q
Whole process						
7.	Observation quality index	—0.01	0.52	0.83	0.50	Yule's Q
8.	Restudies	0.875	0.75	0.835	1.00	Proportion of agreement

a. If we treat Azande as a case report, this becomes statistically significant at 0.05 level by Fisher's Exact Test.
b. One of the cells had no cases; therefore, Yule's Q could not be directly computed; as an approximation, unity was arbitrarily added to the empty cell and Q then computed.
c. Significant at 0.05 level by Fisher's Exact Test
d. Signicant at 0.01 level by Fisher's Exact Test

three of these tests have their chief use in controlling first-stage bias in reports of suicide and homicide. Reports on drunken brawling and witchcraft attribution present little first-stage bias problem. Drunken brawling is a practice that the ethnographer who stays in the field among the people studied for at least a year can reliably report from his own observations independently of informants' statements. Witchcraft attribution for an opposite reason is by definition entirely free of first-stage bias: it concerns itself not with what actually happens but with the mental images of the people. We do not ask how many people are really killed by witchcraft but only how many people are *thought* by the natives to die so.

Test I: Case Reports

This test compares the proportion of "high" and "low" suicide and homicide reports where the ethnographer reported lists of particular cases of suicide or homicide with reports where he did not, but simply generalized that "suicide is rare" or "murder is frequent" or the like. If first-stage bias is exerting an important influence on our statistical arrays because natives tend consistently to overestimate (or underestimate) the frequency of homicide or suicide, in general, then we would expect errors of this sort to be more frequent when the ethnographer does not compile lists of particular cases of suicide or homicide and thus does not place himself in a position to form his own generalization about the frequency of homicide or suicide. (This test would not, however, detect bias which not only distorted the generalization "among us murders are rare" but also affected the classification of a particular event; but this second bias is controlled by Test 2.) Our test results are given in Table 4.

Table 4

Trait	Yule's Q	Significance Level
Defiant homicide	0.33	—
Protest suicide	—0.89	0.05 if Larkin's report on the Azande is treated as a rate report

Test 1 showed a high negative association ($Q = -\ 0.89$) between case reports and reported suicide rates—although not quite statistically significant. On the other hand, no relationship of any significance was found between case reports and reported homicide rates.

A final note. It may be that in checking case reports against generalizations we are checking generalizations made by the ethnographer rather than those made by his informants—ordinarily there is no way to be sure. Ethnographers rarely distinguish generalizations about a culture which they themselves are the first to perceive from generalizations made to them by their informants. It is usual for ethnographers to make no specific acknowledgment of the source of information gotten from informants but instead only to mention the informants in a preface or a footnote if at all. But if our method errs here, it does so on the side of caution; we have another battery of tests to detect bias in the ethnographer's mind.

Test 2: Participant Observation

This test compares the proportion of "high" and "low" reports on all four culture stress indicators where the ethnographer (a) did or (b) did not live among the people studied during the period reported on, so that he could check his informants' statements with his own observations. If first-stage bias is exerting an important influence on our statistical arrays because natives tend to perceive or to remember particular incidents of homicide or suicide erroneously—to form a more comfortable memory, perhaps—then we would expect this influence to be much greater where the ethnographer depends entirely upon his informant's memories than where he can himself observe a death and himself draw conclusions about its circumstances. It does not appear that in fact this bias is strong or important. None of these four tests came near to being statistically significant. Our test results are given in Table 5.

Table 5

Trait	Yule's Q
Drunken brawling	0.38
Defiant homicide	0.00
Protest suicide	0.78
Witchcraft attribution	0.50

See Note b, Table 3.

Another Possible Test: Use of Genealogical Method

A third control test for first-stage bias was thought of too late to apply here but is recommended for future studies of homicide, suicide or witchcraft attribution. That test is the comparison of the proportion of "high" and "low" reports on these indicators where ethnographers (a) did or (b) did not use the genealogical method of study. While this method is usually intended as a tool for the study of kinship patterns, it often involves a systematic check on family deaths which serves as a kind of review of cases and thus a useful check on informants' generalizations.

CONTROLLING SECOND STAGE BIAS (ETHNOGRAPHER'S MIND)

We have three quality control tests on ethnographers' minds and propose a fourth test for future use.

Test 3: Length of Stay

This test compares the proportion of "high" and "low" reports on culture stress indicators made by ethnographers who (a) did or (b) did not stay more than a year among the people. Where observations are carried on by a team who collaborate in the writing of a single research report, the length of stay of each member of the team is added to compute the total length of stay. The longer the ethnographer's mind is exposed to the culture, the more opportunity he has to correct any hastily made erroneous impressions in his mind. The longer he stays, the better he gets to know his informants. The longer he stays, the more chance he has to detect inconsistencies in informants' statements. Thus in general the longer an ethnographer stays in the field, the less likely he is to make erroneous observations of his own and the more likely he is to detect error or deception—especially systematic deception—by an informant.

Most of the reports are only concerned incidentally with the topics that interest us here; usually we have only a few paragraphs to go on. Sometimes, however, the report is a special study of the topic in question: we have the studies of Iroquois suicide by Fenton,[1] Navaho suicide by Wyman and Thorne,[2] Vietnamese suicide by Vu Cong Hoe,[3] Navaho witchcraft by Kluckhohn,[4] and Paiute witchcraft by Beatrice Whiting.[5] Where the indicator whose reliability is being rated is the subject of a separate chapter, article, or monograph, I accept that fact as evidence of a favorable extent of observation even though the author did not spend a year among the people studied.

Where a "favorable" extent of observation obtains, because of a long stay of a single ethnographer, the use of a research team, or the concentration of study upon one of our culture stress indicators, then we would expect informants to be much less frequently successful in deliberately deceiving ethnographers and, similarly, would expect ethnographers to make many fewer errors of direct observation themselves. Consequently, if either of these sources of error, or both together, tend consistently to produce "high" or "low" reports, then this test should show an association between favorable extent of observation and kind of report. In fact, such an association is shown at a 5 per cent level of significance by Fisher's Exact Test between favorable extent of observation and witchcraft attribution reports. This finding thus confirms the basic theory of the quality control test and warns us about a second-stage bias in witchcraft attribution reports (discussed in detail in Chapter 7, below). Our test results are shown in Table 6.

Table 6

Trait	Yule's Q	Significance Level
Drunken brawling	0.22	—
Defiant homicide	0.66	—
Protest suicide	0.29	—
Witchcraft attribution	0.86	0.05

Test 4: Native Language Familiarity

For this study, I deem familiarity by the reporter with the native language a favorable observational condition, and unfamiliarity an unfavorable condition. The degree of familiarity I have in mind does not imply the observer's ability to carry out detailed and subtle lines of inquiry without the aid of an interpreter, but does imply enough knowledge of the language to be aware of its leading concepts and attitudes, to serve as a useful check on an interpreter, and to permit the reporter to converse without the aid of an interpreter when he has to. In practice, I have presumed familiarity where I found evidence that the reporter has conversed at times without an interpreter or evidence that he has made a systematic study of the language (for example, compiled a dictionary or sketched a grammar).

The main reason for including familiarity with native language as an indicator of favorable observational conditions is the superior rapport thus implied. Although in discussing the nuances of witchcraft, at least, native terms for native concepts almost certainly will have to be employed, these terms would naturally come into use even in conversations couched in a contact language. There is no question that a skilled ethnologist can get the information he needs for the culture stress index without a real command of the native language—provided he has adequate rapport, and provided he has the confidence of his informants and can get them to speak freely and honestly. But homicide and witchcraft at least are likely to be delicate topics where rapport is essential. I assume that by and large field workers with some familiarity with the native language have better rapport than those without it.

Accordingly, if informants tend consistently to mislead ethnographers, we would expect this tendency to be smaller among ethnographers who know the native language than among those who do not. We would expect informants to try the deception less often with those who know the language than with those who do not; and we would expect those who do try to succeed less often in their deception. Consequently, we should expect a consistently greater (or smaller, as the case may be) proportion of "high" reports by ethnographers who know the native language than by those who do not. While none of our applications of Test 4 proved statistically significant, both protect suicide and witchcraft attribution associations were high and closely approached significance. Our test results are given in Table 7.

Table 7

Trait	Yule's Q
Drunken brawling	0.25
Defiant homicide	0.71
Protest suicide	0.88
Witchcraft attribution	0.88

Test 5: Ethnographer's Role

I distinguish two kinds of observers whose reports on the indicator traits here considered are assumed to be specially reliable: professional ethnologists and native scholars. A professional ethnologist is defined as a person who makes his living as a teacher or as an expert on ethnology (for example, museum curator) or who is studying to qualify himself for this profession. Ethnology is here loosely used to mean the study of human social or cultural behavior: sociologists, historians, political scientists, economists, social psychologists, geographers, folklorists, jurists, and the like are ethnologists in this sense, as well as anthropologists or ethnologists in the narrow sense. A native scholar is defined as a member of the society whose culture is in question who himself writes a systematic ethnographic report.

On the other hand, reports of professional missionaries or government officials on these indicator traits are assumed to be less reliable. I remember Professor Kroeber's remark about missionaries: "They know more than we do." Both missionaries and government officials have as strong a professional stake as anthropologists in understanding the cultures of the people with whom they work; and usually they spend much longer in the field. However, all of the traits here in question are considered morally wrong either by the people being studied or by the Judeo-Christian moral tradition or by Euro-American legal tradition. Missionaries and government officials alike assume a role of moral authority among the people where they work, and consequently we must suspect a bias on the part of informants, who presumably are less reluctant to talk about such matters freely with anthropologists who are trained to avoid the role of moral authority and eschew all expressions of praise or blame in their talk with informants.

For this test, then, I treat the role of professional ethnologist or of native scholar a favorable observational role and other roles as unfavorable. Our test results are given in Table 8.

Table 8

Trait	Yule's Q
Drunken brawling	—0.28
Defiant homicide	0.00
Protest suicide	0.00
Witchcraft attribution	—0.57

It can be seen at once, however, that this theoretical viewpoint has received no support in its application. Of all the tests for bias used, it alone never attained a measure of association (Yule's Q) greater than 0.60. When we compare its application to witchcraft attribution reports, we find that the other two tests of second-stage bias both showed high positive associations: Test 3 a statistically significant measure, and Test 4 nearly so. Yet this test showed a *negative* association.

Now how are we to explain the fact that while people who stay long in the field are more likely to report high witchcraft attribution rates than people who stay a short time, anthropologists seem less likely to report high witchcraft attribution rates than missionaries. Of the 24 anthropologists who wrote witchcraft attribution reports, and who stated their length of field experience, 11 had spent less than a year in the field while all six of the missionaries who wrote witchcraft attribution reports and stated their length of field experience had spent more than a year in the field. If we compare the reports of anthropologists and missionaries, and control for length of stay, we find the answer: all 11 short-stay authors are anthropologists and *10* of these indicate a low rate of witchcraft attribution while nearly half of the anthropologists who had a long stay indicate a high rate of witchcraft attribution. The contrast is even more striking when we confine our attention to Groups I and III of Table 16, where the reports are explicit and require no adjudication by the comparativist: three of the four long-staying anthropologists report high witchcraft attribution rates, while all four of the short-staying anthropologists report low witchcraft attribution rates. Despite the fact that none of these relationships quite attain statistical significance, we must strongly suspect that anthropologists as a group are less reliable reporters of witchcraft attribution than missionaries and that this difference is a function of their shorter stay in the field. (It may well be associated with a lesser acquaintance with the native language also.)

Another Possible Test: Provenience of Ethnographer

We have not here made any test of theoretical bias on the part of ethnologists. Various theoretical orientations have obtained among field workers at various times. In the seventeenth and eighteenth centuries, two dominant biases were the "savage pagan" bias of traditional European culture and the contradictory "noble primitive" bias of Montaigne and Rousseau. With the emergence of sociology and cultural anthropology as distinct sciences in the nineteenth century, other theoretical orientations became common—classical evolutionist theory in the manner of Comte, Tylor, and Morgan and classical Marxist theory (which accepted Morgan's evolutionism as the theoretical base of ethnological studies); evolutionism was also compatible with nineteenth-century Spencerian social Darwinism, even though the economic implications of this doctrine differed so much from that of Marxism.

Since about 1910, however, three other quite different

theoretical orientations have dominated most anthropological field work outside the Soviet Union. The first of these is "functionalism," in the tradition of Durkheim, Radcliffe-Brown, and Malinowski. The second is "diffusionism," either in the extreme and now discredited tradition of Father Schmidt or the more moderate and entirely respectable tradition of Franz Boas. The third is the "culture-and-personality" school of Sapir, Linton, Benedict, and Mead.

If these theoretical orientations have tended to influence field reports by causing ethnographers to notice and record traits which theory leads them to expect while causing them to overlook and ignore traits which conflict with their theory, we should expect differences in reports published before 1910 (or in the Soviet Union) from reports published after 1910 outside the Soviet Union. This is not to accuse any particular theoretical school of great bias but merely to seek out the unconscious selection bias which may well be found among all. (The importance of this problem and the method of solving it were suggested to me in conversation by William Sewell.)

CONTROLLING THIRD-STAGE BIAS
(COMPARATIVIST'S MIND)

This study, like others before, has several nonstatistical controls for bias in the comparativist's mind. Although the sample studied was not a random sample, nor even a judgmental sample, but rather an opportunistic one, it was chosen not by the comparativist but by Professor Murdock and by contracting officials of the U.S. Government with no special interest in the problem of culture stress. While sampling biases may well exist, they do not reflect the biases of the comparativist's mind. By studying a preselected sample, and reporting all the data therein found on topics defined in advance, the forensic bias of selecting information which supports a special case is cut out.

A second control is afforded by the use of the Human Relations Area Files and the publication in Tables 13 through 16 below of page references to the ethnographical publications relied upon. This control, in its second form a centuries-old hallmark of scholarship, enables a reader to check the accuracy of the comparativist's data compilation quickly and easily. The reader who has access to a set of the files can check the comparativist very quickly indeed; such sets are currently (1960) available for checking at the following universities: Chicago, Colorado, Cornell, Harvard, Hawaii, Indiana, Iowa, Michigan, North Carolina, Oklahoma, Paris (École pratique des hautes études), Pennsylvania, Princeton, Southern California, Southern Illinois, Utah, Washington, and Yale. Data on suicide, homicide, drunken brawling and witchcraft attribution come chiefly from rubrics 682, 762, 733, and 754; data on conditions of observation come chiefly from rubrics 111 and 112. Readers who do not find it convenient to check the comparativist's work in one of these sets of the files can do so somewhat more slowly by looking themselves in the original published reports cited in the tables.

A third control is intended to be afforded by the concept definitions of Chapter 3. In that chapter, I have tried to define the four indicators of culture stress with such precision, detail and objectivity that a field report made with corresponding precision, detail and objectivity can be correctly classified without my judgment intruding. This third control is supposed to reduce the risk of *classification* bias— to reduce the likelihood that the comparativist will slant the results the way he wants them to come out by consciously or unconsciously interpreting imprecise or uncertain reports so as to favor a certain outcome of the study.

Test 6: Explicitness and Generality of Reports

The effectiveness of this third control is formally measured by Test 6. This test compares those reports on one hand that were so explicit in their description and so broad in their generalization that the comparativist had no need to interpret their meaning, no need to us his own judgment in classifying the reported behavior with those reports on the other hand that were either so vague in their description or so restricted in their generalization, or both, that the comparativist did have to use his own judgment. This test assumes that if the comparativist is exerting an interpretive bias, if he is tending to judge all the doubtful cases so as to favor a given outcome—if, in baseball terms, he is an umpire who calls all the close ones in favor of the home team— then this tendency should have wide rein where reports lack either explicitness or generality but should be curbed where they have both. If an ethnographer says: "Suicide is very common among the Wampiwampi; I know of dozens of cases among the 400 villagers I studied" or if he says, "Suicide is unknown among the Wampiwampi; informants are puzzled and shocked by the very concept," the comparativist has no room to intrude a classification bias. Where, however, the ethnographer makes no generalization about the frequency of suicide among the Wampiwampi but discusses circumstances under which it is committed or mentions some illustrative cases, the comparativist has room to intrude bias.

Whiting and Child handled this problem by using several judges who were kept uninformed about the hypotheses being studied to classify the ethnographical reports independently. Whiting and Child then compared the results and computed coefficients of reliability. This method guards against the bias of the comparativist's special thesis and also guards against random error; but it does not guard against other biases in the viewpoint of the judges. Since the judges used in the Whiting and Child study were graduate students in psychology or anthropology, they would be likely to share the prejudices and preconceptions of the academic community to which they and Whiting and Child and you and I belong. Test 6, on the other hand, should detect classification biases of any sort, if they are an important influence on the outcome.

It is also well worth directly comparing the use of the two control methods on witchcraft attribution. Seventeen witchcraft attribution reports used in this study were not clear—either they were vague in description or lacked generality—while 14 were clear, being explicit in description and complete in generalization. Six of the 17 unclear reports were classified by me as reflecting an important role for belief in witchcraft in the society, while 11 were classified by me as reflecting an unimportant role (see Table 16, Chapter 7, below). All but 1 of these 17 cases could be compared with the independent classifications made by B. Whiting [6] or by the judges of Whiting and Child [7]: 7 of these 16 ratings agreed, and 9 disagreed—about what we would expect by chance. Thus considerable error is apparently present in these classifications and it is important to see whether the error is a random one, and thus a benign error, or a consistent bias, and thus a malignant error. Our test results are given in Table 9.

Table 9

Trait	Yule's Q	Significance Level
Drunken brawling	0.50	—
Defiant homicide (see Note b, Table 3)	—0.80	—
Protest suicide	—0.89	0.01
Witchcraft attribution	0.22	—

Test 6 is reassuring as to witchcraft attribution reports: there is obviously no strong classification bias at work there. And as to drunken brawling reports, the test coefficient is moderate and far from statistically significant. We may therefore tentatively conclude that if a classification bias in the comparativist's mind exists at all, it is a rather weak one. However, Test 6 does raise grave doubts about the existence of a serious classification bias in treating defiant homicide reports, whose test coefficient is high and close to statistical significance. This grave doubt about a classification bias in homicide reports is reinforced by the test on suicide reports —here the presence of a bias is clearly indicated at the 1 per cent level of statistical significance. The conclusion seems hard to avoid that in classifying unclear reports of suicide and homicide, I tended consistently to call the doubtful reports "high." Were such a classification error also made with respect to reports about hypothetical culture stress causes, this might well result in spuriously confirming the existence of a relationship which did not in fact exist, or else erroneously rejecting the hypothesis of the existence of a relationship which did in fact exist.

Now this evidence of consistent classification bias is the more important because it is not a self-serving bias. In making this study, I had a personal interest in establishing a variance, in showing that one could classify primitive tribes as either "high" or "low"—that one could tell the high ones from the low ones. That was my thesis and I had a considerable professional stake in the outcome, as do most scientific research workers. The bias here detected actually worked *against* my interests. It is easy to document the existence of the high rates (see Chapter 7 below); the difficult problem is to document the existence of the low. In unconsciously but consistently calling the close ones "high" I was working against my personal interest. Perhaps this bias can be explained as the effect of leaning over backward to avoid biasing the results by making the results come out the way I wanted them to—a bias which is just as serious as and more insidious than the forensic bias. Perhaps it has another cause; if so, independent judges presumably might be also subject to it. Then the method of using independent judges kept ignorant of the research problem would offer no protection: the greater the bias, the higher the likelihood of high coefficients of reliability and hence of spurious statistical reassurances.

CONTROLLING THE WHOLE PROCESS FOR MALIGNANT ERROR (BIAS)

In considering the effects of bias at each stage, one naturally wonders whether the effects tend to cancel each other out or whether instead they are cumulative. Suppose, for example, that informants tend consistently to underestimate homicide rates while ethnographers and comparativists tend consistently to overestimate them; then perhaps the final result will not be far from the truth. But suppose that informants, ethnographers, and comparativists all tend consistently to overestimate suicide rates; then the bias is compounded and the malignancy heighted.

In order to control the cumulative bias of the whole research process, I propose to combine the results in an observation quality index. This index ought to consider each of the factors used in the six control tests so far discussed; however, in this first exploratory study, it was only feasible to use four, the control factors of Tests 2, 3, 4, and 5. In computing the observation quality index, one point is given for a favorable observation condition with respect to each of these four factors. Where more than one independent report is made about an indicator and the reports agree, the results are scored separately and summed—with an extra bonus point being given for the fact of independent corroboration. Where the reports conflict, the results are scored separately and the smaller subtracted from the larger with an extra penalty point subtracted for the fact of conflict.

To illustrate: Vu Cong Hoe's report on Vietnamese suicide [8] is made by a native scholar who has (of course) spent more than a year among his own people; who (of course) speaks the native language; who lives among the people and describes ongoing conditions—OQI score 4. Rivers' [9] classic report on the Toda is written by a professional ethnologist, but one who stayed less than six months in the field, did not learn the native language, and did not claim to live among the people—OQI 1. The data on suicide in Tikopia comes from three sources who are in agreement in suggesting a high rate: Firth [10] (score 4), Rivers [11] (score one point for corroborative testimony and one for ethnologist), and Dillon [12] (one point for corroborative testimony): Tikopia suicide OQI 7. On suicide among the Copper Eskimo, Jenness [13] indicates the rate is low, Rasmussen [14] that it is high; Jenness scores four points, Rasmussen three, so I class the Copper Eskimo suicide rate as low but assign it an OQI of 0.

Validity of the OQI

If the reliability of a particular statement by a particular reporter about a particular people is in doubt, the best way to settle the doubt is to take into consideration everything we know about the reporter, the people, and the topic. An OQI is superfluous.

The function of the OQI is to compare the reliability of the data among statistical arrays. Its assumption is that an array of statements about suicide, homicide, and so on is more likely to be accurate if made by an ethnologist or a native scholar than if made by a missionary or an official, more likely to be accurate if made after a stay of a year than if made after a shorter stay, more likely to be accurate if made by a person familiar with the native language than by one unfamiliar with it, and more likely to be accurate if made as a report of an ongoing way of life by a participant-observer than as a report of a defunct culture or a report by an observer who keeps his distance from the natives.

Obviously, it is arbitrary to equate each of these indicators —their importance varies from culture to culture and from topic to topic. For this reason, I make extensive use of individual indicators as well as of over-all OQI in the quality control tests.

Individual indicators also involve arbitrary judgments: patently a man who has been in the field 366 days does not thereby enjoy an appreciably better observational role than a man who has been in the field 364 days—but the line has to be drawn somewhere.

Furthermore, the indicators measure only those observational characteristics that are easy to make objective judgments about from the kind of data on field methods usually given in field reports. Other factors perhaps even more important go ignored. The personality of the investigator, his attitude toward his work, his training, his skill, and his insights all go unmeasured.

Rivers' book on the Toda [15] has a low OQI, but I agree with the general assessment of the work as a classic of outstanding value. I say again, the purpose of the index is not to rate individual reports but statistical arrays. Rivers' book may be a better book than others written in far more favorable circumstances because Rivers worked harder, had more insight, and was more skillful. But I am not here interested in Rivers' book by itself—only as one of a number of reports on one of a number of peoples. Presumably some other people who worked as hard as Rivers and had as much insight and skill as he also stayed longer, learned the native language, and lived among the people.

Reliability of the OQI

The chief source of information about the conditions of observation has been the "Sources Processed" category (Rubric 111) of the Human Relations Area Files,[16] although other information was used if it happened to turn up. Consequently, some of the sources arc likely to have been underrated: for this as well as other reasons, it would be a gross misapplication of this index to take an individual score as a quality rating of an individual ethnography. An OQI is no substitute for a book review.

It seems to me that the advantage of all four of these criteria is obvious to most field workers and that in field reports of any length or detail they will usually claim credit for them if entitled to them. Usually then, silence about a criterion indicates that the reporter did not enjoy favorable observation conditions.

Test 7: Observation Quality Index (OQI)

If there is a cumulative bias, we would expect this bias to be much more pronounced in reports with a low OQI than in reports with a high OQI. Thus there should be an association (perhaps negative, perhaps positive) between high OQI and high trait reports. Our test results are given in Table 10. (None of these associations are significant by Fisher's Exact Test.) These results entirely reassure us that there is little if any cumulative bias in drunken brawling

Table 10

Trait	Yule's Q
Drunken brawling	—0.01
Defiant homicide	0.52
Protest suicide	0.83
Witchcraft attribution	0.50

reports and suggest that at worst the cumulative bias is moderate in defiant homicide and witchcraft attribution reports; but they warn us that there well may be a serious cumulative bias in protest suicide reports.

CONTROLLING BENIGN ERROR (RANDOM ERROR)

As the reader can see from Tables 13 through 16 of Chapter 7, there were a considerable number of societies where one trait was described independently in two or more ethnographic reports. Usually, though not invariably, these reports not only reflect the work of different ethnographers, but also the use of different informants. Thus they give us an opportunity to measure the effect of random error on the trait reports. Since by definition random error does not reflect any consistent tendency but proceeds from sources as likely to err in one direction as in the other, random errors made by one informant or ethnographer or in one report by the comparativist are independent of those made by another informant or another ethnographer or in another report by the comparativist. If there is a great deal of random error, then we expect a great deal of disagreement between independent reports.

Test 8: Restudies

This test computes the proportion of restudies (second reports) which agree with original studies. The lower the proportion, the more indication of random error we have. (However, should the proportion be much less than half, the hypothesis that the restudies were independent, and hence the test itself, would be discredited). Our test results are given in Table 11. These results are encouraging; and they become more encouraging when it is pointed out that

Table 11

Trait	Number of Restudies	Proportion of Agreement
Drunken brawling	8	0.875
Defiant homicide	4	0.750
Protest suicide	6	0.835
Witchcraft attribution	5	1.000

of the three instances in which restudies were treated as not in agreement, two were doubtful cases, cases of possible conflict, and only one was a case of clear conflict. (Possible conflicts were in the Vietnamese drunken brawling reports and the Iroquois defiant homicide reports; clear conflict was found in Copper Eskimo suicide reports.) The cumulative binomial distribution [17] shows that if the true proportion of disagreements were as great as 0.20 we should expect 95 per cent of random samples of 23 to produce at least two disagreements; if as great as 0.25, at least three disagreements; if as great as 0.30, at least four disagreements. We may tentatively conclude that random error is not a major factor in the data collection process and that no special steps are needed to guard against it. If however we wish to reduce the risk of random error, we could reject field reports which did not present acceptable evidence of care in checking informants' statements and in prompt taking of notes; or we could reject reports unless corroborated by an indepedent observer. Either of these procedures would greatly increase the research effort, since a large proportion of our reports fail to meet either of these tests. Nor does this step seem warranted merely to guard against benign error—especially since pilot studies indicate that relationships of the sort we are interested in are indeed likely to be reported by the kind of study proposed in Chapter 2, above. So we turn from a consideration of control of random error in field reports to that of control of extrapolation error, itself a special kind of random error .

CHAPTER 5

Control of Extrapolation Error

NATURE OF PROBLEM

The comparison of suicide and homicide rates in different groups is complicated by the need to allow for random variation in rate from period to period resulting from chance factors. Failure to make such an allowance may produce grossly misleading deductions. For example, Opler [1] criticizes Winston for extrapolating from Mead's Manu'a data on psychosis to assert an "incidence" rate of 100 psychotics per 100,000. Mead [2] reports two psychotics in a population of 2,000 (describing their symptoms in some detail). What can we conclude about the prevalence of psychosis in Manu'a as compared with that in other populations?

Certainly we cannot, like Winston, simply extrapolate the data and conclude that Manu'a has a higher psychosis rate than any other population with a prevalence under 100 per 100,000. In dealing with small totals, we need to allow for the general tendency of events whose precise time of occurrence is randomly determined to occur not at exactly even

107

intervals but randomly bunched and scattered. We need to allow for this random tendency of timing in the Manu'a data.

The solution is to think of Manu'a as a random sample from an imaginary universe of an infinite number of people living exactly as the Manu'ans do—an imaginary archipelago of Manu'as. On some of these islands there will be more psychotics, and on others less, simply through chance. What can we say about the mean psychosis rate in the universe? This is a simple problem in sampling error of proportion, but one in which the proportion involved is very different from half. Consequently, the instructions usually given in statistics textbooks are inadequate. We do not expect half the people to become psychotic, or to commit suicide or homicide, but only a very small proportion, of the order of 0.001 or less. The appropriate statistic is the cumulative binomial, but since this is not tabulated for proportions this small, we must use approximations. For such proportions, the cumulative Poisson distribution is an approximation whose error is less than 0.001; that is, a calculation using this approximation and reporting a probability of exactly 0.05 that a difference as great as an observed one would occur by chance actually reflects a true probability between 0.049 and 0.051. Where the expected frequency is 100 or less, the cumulative Poisson approximation of the cumulative binomial probability can be directly read from the tables of Molina.[3] Where the expected frequency is over 100, the normal approximation to the cumulative binomial can be used, with an error ranging downward from 0.00254.[4] Neither of these approximations assume normal distribution; they are nonparametric statistics which assume only that the probabilities of the events do not change from one event to the next and that each event occurs independently of every other. (But a suicide pact or a mass murder would have to be counted as but one case, since the suicides or the murders would not have occurred independently.)

This method of imaginary universes use sampling theory as a yardstick of plausibility to test a special kind of null hypothesis. Ordinarily, sampling theory seeks to make possible inferences about a real universe from a random sample. Here sampling theory is used instead to test the hypothesis that actual differences in total rates of suicide or homicide between two small universes do not reflect differences in the conditions of life there but only differences in random bunching or scattering of these phenomena. If this null hypothesis is plausible, then the differences are of such a magnitude as would occur if the two populations studied were random samples from a single large universe. To test this null hypothesis, then, all that we have to do is to test the hypothesis that two populations (which in fact are entire small universes) differ in psychosis rate to a greater extent than we would expect from two random samples of these sizes from a large population. If they do differ to this extent, our conclusion is not the usual one—that they did not in fact come from the same population. We already knew that they did not in fact do so. Instead, our conclusion is that they differ so much in psychosis (or suicide or homicide) rate that the conditions of life affecting this rate must likewise be different. Here sampling theory is used as a model of measurement of the occurrence of random scattering and bunching—sampling theory is used as a yardstick to measure not samples but entire small universes.

CONTROL OF RANDOM ERROR

Individual Observations

The suicide and homicide tables below show for each people a plausible rate of protest suicide and defiant homicide. In each case, we are interested in knowing how great a difference in observed incidence of suicide and homicide is needed to make plausible an inference that the true rate differs from the base rate—10 per 100,000 per year (10 per 2,000 per 50-year period) for suicide, half that for homicide. Where statements imply the total number of events occurring within the memory of living informants, we take the period involved to be 40 years where low rates are reported, or 80 years where high rates are reported; that is, we assume that living memory extends at least 40 years back but no longer than 80 years.

Consider the Copper Eskimo, in all about 800 people. How small a suicide report would assert a true rate of less than 10 suicides per 2,000 people per 50-year period? That is, how small a rate would be likely to occur by chance in a random sample of 800 people from an infinite universe whose rate is 10 per 100,000 per year? The rate of 10 suicides per 2,000 people per 50 years is equivalent to 3.23 suicides per 800 people per 40 years. Hence the expected frequency is 3.23; the Molina tables [5] show that with such an expected frequency, a result as small as zero (no suicides at all) would occur by chance about 4 per cent of the time. Thus a difference this great in either direction would occur by chance about 8 per cent of the time. On individual extrapolation computations, I am willing to accept the 5 per cent level of significance; at that level there is no rate small enough to be plausible evidence that the true rate of suicide among the Copper Eskimo is less than the base rate of 10 per year per 100,000 (10 per 50 years per 2,000); consequently, in the "Plausible Incidence" column of Table 15, I have entered "absent." Or consider the Toda: there we have data derived from a thorough genealogical study extending over four generations, which we take as 80 years; for approximately 600 Toda we have a report of three suicides; assuming a true rate of 10 per 100,000, a total incidence as small as 1 would occur through random sampling error (as shown by a computation like that for the Copper Eskimo) in less than 25 samples out of 1,000; hence we table the plausible rate for the Toda as 1. Since in fact the rate is 3, here again the hypothesis that the observed difference could be explained as a mere random scatter is not rejected. But when we consider the Apayao, who number about 11,000, then the plausible incidence in 40 years from this point of view proves from a like calculation to be 31 or less; and since Vanoverbergh's[6] informants could recall only one such suicide the hypothesis that this low a report reflects a mere random scatter can be decisively rejected as utterly implausible. Similarly, for the 245 Harney Valley Paiute, a suicide incidence as great as 6 cannot plausibly be explained as a mere random bunch, and B. Whiting[7] reports a total of 23.

Arrays

As already said, if the arrays correlate significantly with those of other variables as hypothesized, all is well. The comparativist examines the evidence for extrapolation error and the *more* such evidence, the *higher* he estimates the true correlation. However, if the result fails to correlate significantly as hypothesized, but does indicate a good possibility that this failure results from random error—if the correlations are in the direction predicted and almost but not quite statistically significant—then the comparativist may regret that he had not taken steps to reduce random error before computing his correlations. He may regret that he had not dropped from his sample those reports which seemed most likely to reflect random error rather than true variance. If he drops some now and tests for correlation, and if he is again unsuccessful, perhaps drops some more and tries again, he is indulging in the naive fallacy of hunting through data for correlations rather than reporting whether correlations occur as predicted. The odds against dealing any given bridge hand at cards are very large; every bridge deal involves a most unlikely arrangement. Nothing is learned by pointing out after the deal that the arrangement is most improbable. On the other hand, very much would be learned from a showing that through extrasensory perception it is possible to predict in advance of the deal the way the four hands will turn out.

Whatever decision the comparativist makes about controlling extrapolation error, he must make it in advance. He can decide to do nothing at all; if his correlations come out significant anyway, he is all right. But where he wishes to guard against the risk of seriously lowering his correlations by extrapolation error, his obvious course is to decide in advance to accept only reports some minimum distance from the base value, that is, to fix some maximum acceptable probability that a rate results from random extrapolation error. For example, suppose he fixed the distance at one probable error. Then he decides in advance to reject any high rate unless rates that high would be expected to occur through chance less than 25 per cent of the time and to reject any low rate unless rates that low would be expected to occur through chance less than 25 per cent of the time. Following this procedure, he would accept a report of a suicide incidence of 1 among the Copper Eskimo, since that small an incidence would occur by chance in less than 19 per cent of samples made from a universe with a true rate of 10 per 100,000 per year, but would reject a report of an incidence of 2, since that small an incidence would occur by chance in over 37 per cent of the samples. He would accept a report of a suicide incidence of 3 among the Toda since that small an incidence would occur in less than 25 per cent of the samples, but would reject a report of 4 since that small an incidence would occur by chance in 29 per cent of the samples.

CONTROL OF BIAS

No bias arises from smallness of population. Extrapolation error is as likely to occur in one direction as the other. However, in conversation with one highly sophisticated sociologist, I heard the contrary. My colleague argued that a bias was introduced, because small populations might well have true suicide or homicide rates differing from large populations simply because they were small—because the conditions of life in a small population differ from the conditions of life in a large population. Such differences would certainly seem plausible from Redfield's folk-urban continuum theory.[8] My own cross-cultural survey of social development[9] and field work in a Tyrolean peasant community satisfy me that Redfield's theory is substantially sound. Conditions of life in small communities do differ because they are small from conditions of life in large communities.

But this is beside the point. If in fact suicide rates are higher (or lower) in small communities than in large ones, a cross-cultural survey using the controls for random extrapolation error just described can be expected to so report. Such a difference would not be an observation error but a sociological fact.

In discussing the imaginary universe—the imaginary

archipelago of Manu'as, for example—it must be borne in mind that such a universe is thought of as an infinite number of peoples living under exactly the same circumstances as the real population at hand. Thus the people on each of the imaginary Manu'as need to be imagined as inhabiting an imaginary Samoa in an imaginary Pacific Ocean on an imaginary earth, entirely out of touch with and unaware of each of the other imaginary Manu'as.

CHAPTER 6

Control of Population Estimates

This chapter demonstrates a new method of testing for the occurrence of *serious error* in population estimates. By *serious error* is meant error so large, so frequent or so systematic as to produce misleading conclusions about the problem being studied—in this work, misleading conclusions about rates of suicide or homicide.

Since both protest suicide and defiant homicide ratings concern themselves with rates, it is not enough to estimate the frequency of suicides and homicides; we must also estimate the size of population involved. Furthermore, since in many cases the rate estimates involve periods of 40 to 80 years, we must then estimate the average population over a 40- to 80-year period. How reliable are the population estimates on which we base our calculations? Table talk among anthropologists shows a widespread belief that population reports of primitive people are so unreliable as to be practically worthless unless the report is based on a census taken under the supervision of an anthropologist. The data quality control tests in this chapter provide substantial support for the contrary view, that existing population estimates are reliable enough to be useful in research. I show that there is no reason to believe a major systematic bias occurs in these estimates—that there is no general tendency to undershoot or overshoot the mark widely. I show that the variance (spread of estimates) is comparable for official censuses and rough estimates. Consequently, it seems reasonable to infer that while individual errors of a magnitude of ± 20 per cent are doubtless common enough, the estimate process is in working control. (By *working control* is meant a state of data observation conditions such that random errors and bias are kept within acceptable limits.)

The method of quality control used here depends upon the differences in type and magnitude of error to be expected among the three leading types of population estimate. Ethnographic censuses are taken as the standard of reliability against which government censuses are measured for systematic bias; it is assumed that there is no over-all tendency of any importance for ethnographic censuses as a class of observations consistently to underestimate or consistently to overestimate populations. Censuses of either kind are taken as a standard of reliability for random error; rough estimates are compared with censuses to control random error.

TYPES OF ESTIMATES

Ethnographic censuses are those in which the enumerator is a professional ethnologist who enumerates a community as part of a community study. He may get this data by interviews with members of each household or instead with key informants who know the entire community. For communities up to one or two thousand people this method is accurate. The ethnologist has a strong professional stake in accuracy. The ethnologist is dealing with a community where a number of the older informants know personally every member. He himself gets to know many households and can check his informants and his data against genealogies. He likewise gets to know the kinship system and general way of life of the people, so that he can avoid errors or oversights arising from ignorance of a strange culture pattern. He has rapport with his informants and poses no threat of tax raises, military service or other possible concomitants of an official census.

It is to be expected that ethnographic censuses have the least error, either random or bias. Only one people in this sample has been twice enumerated by ethnographers—the Copper Eskimo. Jenness [1] about 1915 counted 800 people, Rasmussen [2] in 1923 counted 816—a difference of only 2 per cent in seven or eight years, all of which might plausibly be explained as natural increase.

Official censuses are those in which the enumerators are people specially enlisted for the purpose of taking a census sponsored by political authorities. Sometimes the enumerators are special employees hired for a few weeks and perhaps given a brief course of instruction. Sometimes they are administrative officials given the enumeration task in addition to their other duties. They may interview a member of each household, or may instruct the head of each household to file an oral or written report. Usually, enumerators in official censuses do not have a strong professional stake in accuracy and no doubt often are tempted to guess at some data or to wink at the exclusion of some households or even local groups in order to save themselves trouble. If, as is so often true with the peoples in this sample, the enumerators belong to a different culture from the enumerated people, they are likely to misunderstand descriptions of household membership where kinship systems and residence attitudes differ from their own. The enumerator rarely has time to gain the confidence of his informants, to gain rapport. Informants may rightly or wrongly believe that their interest lies in concealing the true size of their household in order to lessen its burden of taxes or military or labor service.

Rough estimates are usually based on a formal or informal dwelling count or estimate. The evidence from this sample presented below fails to support the hypothesis that rough estimates are any less reliable than official censuses. This should not be so surprising. After all, most of the sources of error involved in counting people are avoided in counting dwellings, and only a little first-hand acquaintance with native settlements enables an observer to make a fairly good estimate of the average number of people per dwelling.

CONTROL OF BIAS

Is there a consistent bias in government censuses? Table talk among anthropologists shows that many of them think censuses of primitive peoples by colonial powers generally tend to underestimate the population. The present sample offers 12 comparisons between official censuses and ethnographic censuses: in 7 of these pairs (found among the Timbira, the Toda, and the Ifalik) the official census is lower than the ethnographic census; in 5 of these pairs (found among the Pukapuka and the Omaha) it is higher. (In none of these pairs was the ethnographic return more than half again as great as the official return.) The nonparametric sign test shows that differences this great would arise through chance more than 25 per cent of the time.[3] Consequently I do not accept the hypothesis that there is a serious bias in official censuses. The ethnographic censuses in this sample are too few for us to compare variance between official censuses and ethnographic censuses, but it can hardly be doubted that the former have a much higher level of random error than the latter.

Does a comparison of census and rough estimates of the same people yield any indication of bias? Among 6 peoples of our sample comparisons are possible with the data at hand: in 3 of these, government censuses ran lower than rough estimates; in the other 3 they ran higher. The hypothesis of serious difference is not supported.

Making use of the population data available not only in the Human Relations Area Files [4] but also in Swanton [5] and Steward [6] on the peoples in our sample where useful reports were found on either homicide or suicide, I have tested the hypothesis that there is serious bias in official censuses and rough estimates. The tests have failed to support this hypothesis. The samples in these tests are too small to warrant the conclusion that *no* biases exist, but they are large enough to warrant the conclusion that the differences between high rates and low rates of suicide and homicide in Tables 14 and 15 of Chapter 7 cannot be plausibly explained as the effect of bias in population estimate.

CONTROL OF RANDOM ERROR

The problem here is much like that of controlling for extrapolation error, though the statistical methods differ. I consider first whether random error differs among rough estimates and censuses and then go on to discuss the control of random errors in individual estimates and arrays.

As already explained in the discussion of extrapolation error, we are interested in many cases here in 40- or 80-year periods. In comparing population estimates, it is not possible to separate variance in rate of change of population from variance in estimate error, because successive estimates are almost always made some years apart. The unit of comparison is the pair of estimates: the statistic compared is the mean annual change of the common logarithm of population. (To illustrate: according to an 1806 census, Aleut population was 1,953 people; according to an 1818 census, 1,469 people. Since population changes at an exponential rate, the average annual change should be computed in logarithms. The common logarithm of 1,953 is 3.291; of 1,469 is 3.167, a decrease of 0.124. So the mean annual change of the logarithm of population is one-twelfth of 0.124, or 0.0103.)

Comparison of these ACLP (annual change of the logarithm of population) means simultaneously tests two hypotheses: (1) that by and large true rates of population change among people enumerated by censuses differ from rates of change among people enumerated by rough estimates (after all, it could be argued a priori that in fact a rapid rate of change might be more likely to stimulate a special rough estimate than a special census and hence that in fact peoples enumerated by rough estimates might have by and large a faster rate of change than peoples enumerated by censuses); (2) that random error or variance of rough estimates differs from random error or variance of censuses—the hypothesis which really interests us.

I have computed a total of 33 such ACLP means. Twenty-two of them involve two government censuses (official ACLP means); the other 11 involve at least one rough estimate (rough ACLP means). These reports come from 11 peoples in the sample, three of which contribute both official and rough ACLP means.

The grand mean of the 11 rough ACLP means is 0.006678; that of the 22 official ACLP means is 0.006956. Assuming normal distribution, a difference between means this great would occur in 89 per cent of random samples through mere chance. Thus the hypothesis that there is a difference between these means is not supported. There is a difference in the variance of ACLP means of the sample: the standard error of the official means is 0.00702; that of the rough means is 0.00407. Assuming normal distribution, a difference this great would occur by chance in more than 5 per cent but less than 10 per cent of random samples.[7] Thus, if anything, the results of this test support the hypothesis that rough estimates have a smaller random error than government censuses—or else that later rough estimates may tend to be influenced by earlier ones. But neither test reaches the 1 per cent level of confidence; we do not accept the hypothesis that there is a serious difference. By methods that assume normal distribution of the logarithms of the means of population estimates, I have tested the hypotheses that random errors of means or variances of population rough estimates differ seriously from those of population censuses. Neither test proved significant; consequently, less sensitive non-parametric tests would presumably likewise fail to report a significant difference. However, these results do alert us to the possibility that perhaps variances among censuses may be *greater* than those among rough estimates.

In preparing the Plausible Incidence column of Tables 14 and 15, I have also considered the plausibility of the hypothesis that the difference between the reported incidence and the base rate is to be explained as a reflection of random error in population estimates. This test was not made where the populations were so large that the *annual* rate of suicide or homicide is tabled, but only where living memory calculations were involved, since for them I have had to estimate the often considerable changes in population over a 40- or 80-year period. For living memory calculations, wherever at least three population estimates were available, at least one of which was made in the first half of the period in question and at least one in the second half, the ACLP mean was computed for all possible pairs of early and late estimates. The mean and standard deviation of these ACLP means were computed and using Student's t the 95 per cent two-tailed confidence limits of the ACLP means were computed. This method assumes normal distribution, but in it moderate departures from normality are unimportant.[8] Furthermore, random errors may plausibly be assumed to take a substantially normal distribution. From the limit less favorable to the hypothesis that the reported suicide or homicide rate differs from the base rate, the expected frequency was recomputed. In only one case, the Aleut, did this procedure yield a more extreme plausible incidence than the extrapolation computation. The Plausible Incidence column, then, shows the minimum (maximum) incidence of low (high) reports needed to refute at the 5 per cent level of confidence the hypothesis that the reported differences from the base rate reflect either extrapolation error or population estimate error.

Control of random error of these estimates in arrays follows the same principles as control of random error from extrapolation, already discussed. To reduce the error, the comparativist should survey his arrays before computing correlations and reject items with more than an acceptable chance (for example, more than 50 per cent chance) of being mere reflections of population estimate error.

Indeed, he should reject items where there is more than a 50 per cent chance that the reported difference of the rate from the base value reflects either population estimate error or extrapolation error or both. Let x = probability that difference in reported rate from base rate results from random error in population estimate. Let y = probability that this difference results from random extrapolation error. Then it follows from a well-known theorem in probability mathematics [9] that the combined probability that this difference results from *either one* of these is given by the formula $x + y - xy$. Table 12 shows the maximum acceptable probabilities such that $a + b - ab = 0.50$.

Table 12

a	b
0.50	0.00
0.40	0.16
0.30	0.28
0.29	0.29
0.20	0.37
0.10	0.44
0.00	0.50

Application of Controls to Culture Stress Indicators

This chapter uses all of the techniques presented thus far here to evaluate the trustworthiness and reliability of the four indicators of culture stress proposed and defined in Chapter 3. For each indicator I present a summary of the statistical quality control tests; these formally test for bias and random error. Furthermore, I discuss in detail all specific problems of comparativist's interpretation, in a further effort to control for bias in comparativist's inferences. I present a table which gives among other things specific page references to the sources of the data, so that the work can readily be checked. These tables also show the observation quality index (OQI) of each society. The tables on protest suicide and defiant homicide offer further control data: The Plausible Inference column (captioned PI) shows the minimum (maximum) number of suicides or homicides needed to make plausible at the 5 per cent level of confidence an inference of high (low) protest suicide or defiant homicide rate, considering both the factor of extrapolation error discussed in Chapter 5 and that of

125

population estimate error discussed in Chapter 6. Where it is feared that the size of population might influence an ethnographer's estimate of the frequency of a trait, the data are tabulated separately for large (over 10,000 population) and small societies, in order to control for that factor. (Indeed, even though not included in Table 3 or discussed in Chapter 4 above or further below, control tests were made for relationship between total population and high trait reports on all four traits. These tests all produced Q coefficients smaller than $\pm$ 0.66, and none approached statistical significance; hence the intrusion of bias in observer's estimate as an artifact of population size is in working control for all four indicators.)

Furthermore, in the discussion of defiant homicide and protest suicide, I assemble selected evidence for the proposition that there is a true variance in these traits—in other words, that the wide differences in reported rates must reflect something else besides reporting errors, must reflect at least in part underlying differences in actual homicide and suicide incidence. This demonstration seems necessary because otherwise the generally untrustworthy nature of these reports might leave some room for the belief that there might actually be no variance at all in suicide or homicide rates from society to society. A basic thesis of this study concerning these rates is that while reported suicide and homicide rates may well reflect many distortions due to reporting bias or random error, *one* of the factors importantly influencing the reported frequency of each is the true frequency. To buttress this proposition, I sought widely data that would tend to make implausible the hypothesis that all apparent differences in suicide rates were functions of reporting error and tend instead to show that the existing evidence compels the inference that there must be some real variance in the actual rates. Another reason for being interested in the extent of the true variance is the fact that the greater the true variance the more room there is for error before a true "high" rate is erroneously reported as a "low" rate or vice versa.

CONTROL OF THE DRUNKEN BRAWLING INDICATOR

Table 13 shows the data on drunken brawling. The column captioned OQI shows the total observation quality

Table 13—Frequency of Drunken Brawling

People	OQI	Reporter
	GROUP I—DRUNKEN BRAWLING FREQUENT	
	Population over 10,000	
Ojibwa, ca. 1940	1	#Kinietz 1947:140
Iroquois, ca. 1800, 1900–1940	6	#Fenton 1941: passim; #Parker 1913:20f
Navaho, ca. 1932	3	#Van Valkenburgh 1936:52; #Hrdlicka 1908:169
Cuna, ca. 1680	3	#Wafer 1934:91f; #DePuyt 1868; (#Stout 1947:94f)
Tupinamba, ca. 1662	1	#Cardim 1906:421; #Heriarte 1847:16
Chagga women, ca. 1910	3	#Gutmann 1926:161f
Azande, ca. 1885	*	#Casati 1891:248; (Czekanowsky 1924:29f)
Vietnamese (Cochin China), ca. 1865	1	#Richard 1867:111
Central Bisayans, ca. 1945	1	Martin Reif Ms. from informant in Los Angeles, U.S.A., and memory of field trip
Apayao, ca. 1930	3	#Vanoverbergh 1936–1938:161
	Population under 10,000	
Aleut, ca. 1873, 1937	5	#Elliot 1886:136f; #Hrdlicka 1945:95
Northern Paiute, ca. 1937	2	#Whiting 1950:61
Southeast Salish, ca. 1929	2	#Ray 1933:112
Siriono, ca. 1931	2	#Holmberg 1950:37–39, 62
Omaha, ca. 1880	3	#Dorsey 1896:370
Carib, ca. 1932	2	#Gillin 1936:19, 61, 65

Table 13—Frequency of Drunken Brawling (Cont.)

GROUP II—INTOXICANTS USED BUT BRAWLING RARE OR ABSENT

Population over 10,000

Jivaro, ca. 1928	1	# Brüning 1928:55; (# Karsten 1935:121)
Ashanti, ca. 1922	3	# Rattray 1923:135; # Rattray 1929:329
Cambodia, ca. 1886	2	# Maurel 1887:316; # Thompson 1937:348
Hainan, ca. 1942	1	# Odaka 1950:27f, 60
Vietnamese, ca. 1927	2	# Gourou 1936:460, 525-8; (Robequain 1939:277)
Ifugao, ca. 1939	4	# Daguio 1952:27; (# Barton 1922:407)

Population under 10,000

Ifalik, ca. 1947	3	# Burrows 1949:30
Timbira, ca. 1933	3	# Nimuendaju 1946:129, 160
Toda, ca. 1901	1	# Rivers 1906:476, 455

GROUP III—REPORTS INCONCLUSIVE
Intoxicants Used but No Data on Brawling

Chagga men, Khasi, Laos, Miao, Mbundu, Tanala, Thonga, Tiv

No Intoxicants Used

Copper Eskimo, Tikopia

See Table 14 for explanation of captions and entries.

index of the report on each people. Reports on societies with large populations (over 10,000) are listed separately from reports on societies with small total populations (under 10,000) in order to show whether there is any tendency for drunken brawling to be more frequently reported from large populations than from small ones; if there were such a tendency, it would suggest that the purported differences in drunken brawling frequency merely reflect the size of population studied. However, no such tendency does exist in these reports; the Q coefficient is obviously and gratifyingly nonsignificant — 0.02). I now review the statistical quality control tests and discuss in detail the possibility that I as comparativist may have introduced a bias into the work.

Statistical Quality Control Tests

None of the statistical quality control tests on drunken brawling reports give any reason for serious concern. None of the Q coefficients are higher than 0.50; all but one are below 0.40. The absence of any important bias in the minds of informants on drunken brawling is indicated by Test 2, which failed to show any significant relationship between use of participant-observation field methods by ethnographer and high reports of drunken brawling ($Q = 0.38$). The absence of any important bias affecting drunken brawling reports in the minds of ethnographers is indicated by Tests 3, 4, and 5: Test 3 failed to show any significant relationship between ethnographer's length of stay in the field and high drunken brawling reports ($Q = 0.22$); Test 4 failed to show any significant relationship between ethnographer's familiarity with the native language and high drunken brawling reports ($Q = 0.25$); Test 5 failed to show any significant relationship between high drunken brawling reports and ethnographer's role (professional social scientist or native scholar treated as "favorable" roles; others as "unfavorable") $Q = -0.28$). The absence of a serious bias affecting interpretation of vague or ungeneralized drunken brawling reports in the mind of the comparativist in indicated by Test 6: no significant relationship appears between explicitness and generality of reports and their classification by me as "high" or "low" ($Q = 0.50$). The absence of a cumulative bias involving the first two stages of the ethnological research process seems practically certain: no relationship at all appears between observation quality index (OQI) and high drunken brawling reports ($Q = -0.01$). Nor is there any reason to fear extensive random error: of the eight societies for which we have more than one independent report on drunken brawling, seven sets of reports are in agreement; the eighth, on Vietnam, may or may not reveal a true conflict, since the two reports in apparent conflict refer to different regions of Vietnam and different periods of time (details below). To sum up, I have systematically studied 36 field reports on 25 societies. From this examination, I found no indication of a bias in drunken brawling reports. It is true that the total number of reports studied is rather small; but from the same sample we find considerable reason to suspect bias in the other indicators studied; the fact that all six tests for bias were reassuring is an additional reason for doubting that there is any serious or important bias in ethnological field reports on drunken brawling.

Bias in Comparativist's Inferences

Seven of the high reports reflect a generalization by a field worker that drunken brawling is a regular occurrence (Ojibwa, Tupinamba, Azande, Apayao, Northern Paiute, Siriono, Carib); an eighth reflects a similar generalization made to Martin Reif[1] (my research assistant) by a Central Bisayan informant in Los Angeles and confirmed by Reif's memory of his own observations while on military service in this area during World War II. Among seven other peoples, drunkenness is stated to be common and specific incidents of brawling are reported (Navaho, Cuna, Iroquois, Chagga [women], Aleut, Southeast Salish, and Omaha). The quarrels reported include murders among the Navaho, Salish, and Omaha and stabbing among the Cuna. (Perhaps it would produce more reliable classification if drunken brawling were reconceptualized as regular drunkenness accompanied either by regular physical assaults or by any drunken homicides within living memory.)

Two low reports reflect explicit generalizations of ethnographers that while the people often get drunk, drunkenness never results in violence (Ifugao, Ifalik). Of a third, Rivers[2] reports that he has seen Toda drunk on occasion but knows of no physical assaults under these circumstances or any other circumstances except in connection with a forcible transfer of wives. Nimuendaju[3] reports that although the Timbira commit unspecified "misdeeds" while drunk, they have a general aversion to disputes; if we follow the legal rule of construing the two statements to avoid inconsistency, we would infer that the "misdeeds" in question do not involve disputes but instead other behavior disapproved by the Timbira. Of the Cambodians, I have no data about disputes, only evidence that drunkenness was very rare in the late nineteenth century; Maurel[4] so reports at the time and Thompson[5] 50 years later reports that recently drunkenness has become more common, while formerly rare.

On three peoples, the reports are equivocal and I have had to guess: while many reporters attest the frequency of drunkenness among the Jivaro, Brüning[6] remarks that he has heard of "occasional brawls between drunken Indians"—on balance, considering the large number of Jivaro and Jivaro communities, and the failure of other reporters to say anything about brawls while emphasizing the importance of drinking, I have hesitantly concluded that brawling is infrequent. The Hainanese drink during feasts—there is a two-week celebration at the New Year—but Odaka[7] says that they do not drink "excessively" and that "one who drinks without self-control is ridiculed by the villagers as a loafer." Again on balance the report suggests to me the absence of brawling.

The Vietnamese present a special problem of inference: Gourou[8] reports observations made 1927–1930 that the Vietnamese are much given to drinking but little given to brawling; Richard [9] more than half a century earlier reported frequent public brawling among Vietnamese women. Two plausible explanations present themselves for this conflict: (1) Customs may have changed in the sixty years; women may have stopped public brawling. (2) Richard worked in Cochin China in South Vietnam; Gourou worked in the delta of Tonkin in North Vietnam; there may be regional differences. (It is worth remarking that while local peasant dialects of Vietnamese in Tonkin differ to the point of mutual unintelligibility from those in Annam [Central Vietnam], Tonkinese and Cochin Chinese dialects are mutually intelligible, the latter having been settled by sea from more distant Tonkin rather than by land from the nearer Annam.) I have tabulated Vietnamese *ca.* 1865 in Group I, and Vietnamese *ca.* 1927 in Group II.

The Ashanti present another special problem. They certainly use alcoholic drinks. They have a rule that drunkenness may be taken as extenuating circumstances in the judgment of many legal offenses, but not in the murder of a chief. Rattray [10] says that in general "the Ashanti are not very prone to come to blows in their disputes, which are, for the most part, wordy duels." Considering this generalization, the large number of the Ashanti, and the substantial development of their law courts, which would tend to preserve a rule about drunkenness and murders whether or not incidents had taken place in living memory, I have hesitantly tabled the Ashanti in Group II.

In all, eight high reports and three low reports involve no judgments of any kind by me as comparativist. Three other high reports reflect drunken homicides and a fourth drunken stabbing; reconceptualization of drunken brawling could make these three or four more direct reports.

CONTROL OF THE DEFIANT HOMICIDE INDICATOR

Table 14 shows the data on defiant homicide. I do not claim that the Reported Rate column accurately reflects the true rate. I do claim that most of the rate reports above five and most of the vague reports labeled "Rate Seems High" come from societies where the true rate of defiant homicide is higher than that in most societies with rate reports below five or vague reports labeled "Rate Seems Low." In support of this view, I begin by marshaling evidence that there really is a variance in the true rates of defiant homicide—that homicide is in fact more common in some communities than in others of the same size. Next I consider whether any inferences of mine about the data have introduced a bias. And finally I discuss the quality control tests on the field reports.

Existence of Variance

I begin by examining evidence both from my sample and from outside it to show beyond doubt that true differences in homicide rates occur—that there is a variance. Beatrice Whiting [11] describes in detail five case histories of homicide among about 250 Harney Valley Paiute, and Ray [12] lists six homicides among 486 Sanpoil (Southeast Salish); a true frequency of four or more provides plausible evidence for the Harney Valley Paiute, and one of six or more for the Sanpoil. If we examine the reports of government statistical bureaus as compiled in the 1956 *United Nations Demographic Yearbook* [13] (considering only the most trustworthy category of reports) we find five reports above per 100,000: Southwest African Whites (6.0), Trinidad and Tobago (6.5), Alaska (7.2), Union of South Africa Colored (15.2), and Taiwan (21.5). I do not suggest that any of these UN reports are

Table 14—Defiant Homicide Reports

People	OQI [a]	Reporter [b]	RR [c]	IR [d]	PI [e]	Population [f]
		RATE REPORTS				
Paiute (Harney Valley) 1856–1935	2	Whiting 1950:62f, 76–78	>25.5	>5	4	245
Southeast Salish (Sanpoil) 1851–1930	2	#Ray 1933:112	15.4	6	6	486
Navaho (reservation only), ca. 1936 [g]	2	#Van Valkenburgh 1936:52	14.5	5	6	34,444
Toda, 1862–1901	1	#Rivers 1906:554f	<3.0	0	absent	670
Siriono, 1902–1942 [h]	2	#Holmberg 1950:60f	1.3	1	0	1,560
Aleut, 1795–1835	3	#Veniaminov 1840a:55	<1.2	0	1	1,670
Tanala, ca. 1926	1	#Linton 1933:155	<1.0	0	4	209,954
Miao, ca. 1937	1	#Hudspeth 1937:43f	<1.0	1	3	

VAGUE REPORTS

Rate Seems High—Population below 10,000

People	OQI	Reporter			PI	Population
Copper Eskimo 1836–1916	7	#Jenness 1922:88f, 94f; #Stefansson 1913:289f			8	807
Omaha, 1835–1905	3	#Dorsey 1896:370; (#Fletcher and LaFleche 1911: 618f)			11	1,215

Rate Seems High—Population above 10,000

People	OQI	Reporter			PI	Population
Tupinamba, 1582–1662 [i]	2	#Heriarte 1847:16; #Cardim 1906:421			181	**39,000**
Tiv, ca. 1936	4	#East 1939:260f			40	560,000
Khasi, ca. 1910?	2	#Stegmiller 1924:32–42; (#Gurdon 1907:5)			16	200,000

Rate Seems Low—Population above 10,000

People	OQI	Reporter			PI	Population
Ojibwa, 1895–1935	2	#Landes 1937:109; #Kinietz 1947:140-2			45	30,000
Iroquois, 17th century (??) [j]	1	#Morgan 1901:133, 321; but compare #Fenton 1941:90, 120f.			13	**12,000**
Cuna (San Blas) 1900–1940	3	#Stout 1947:30f			21	**16,000**
Laos, ca. 1935 [k]	0	#Thompson 1937:365			48	1,260,000

Table 14—Defiant Homicide Reports (Cont.)

UNCLASSIFIABLE REPORTS

Rate Seems Less than 9 per 100,000

| Timbira, 1893–1933 | 3 | # Nimuendaju 1946:159 | **299** |
| Ifalik, 1909–1948 | 2 | # Spiro 1950:203 | 304 |

Defiant Homicide Occurs—No Suggestion of Rate

Aranda, Apayao, Ashanti, Azande, Carib (Barama River), Chagga, Ifugao, Korea, Mbundu; Pukapuka, Rwala, Samoa.

    a. Observation Quality Index: the numerals are index scores.
    b. Source and page number, for full citation see bibliography. Sources marked #
were consulted in the Human Relations Area Files. Sources entered in parentheses are
either (a) too vague in themselves to imply a high or low rate but tend to support the
other source(s) relied on and are therefore cited for information; or (b) secondary sources
who may be following the same primary source already used by me. Sources entered
in parentheses are *not* counted in the OQI computation.
    c. Reported Rate. Generally computed by me from reported incidence and mean
population.
    d. Incidence Report. Number of homicides reported.
    e. Plausible Incidence. Minimum (maximum) number of suicides needed to make
plausible an inference of high (low) protest suicide rate, considering both extrapolation
error and standard error of mean of population estimates (see Chapters 5 and 6 for
detailed discussion).
    f. For annual rates (used where populations exceeded 50,000), this is the geometric
mean of available estimates. For living memory rates, unless in heavy type, this is the
mean of estimates of population at the middle of the period concerned, computed from
ACLP means of all available combinations of early and late estimates, the annual change
being interpolated between the two estimates; for living memory rates where this procedure could not be followed, the geometric mean of available estimates is tabled and
the entry set in heavy type. (See text for detailed discussion.)
    g. The Navaho data concerns only Navaho living on the Navaho reservation, and
excludes about 10,000 Navaho living off the reservation (mostly in northwestern New
Mexico).
    h. The Siriono computation is based on the whole Siriono population, although
Holmberg only worked with one band of about 90 people; the assumption is that this
band was in touch with others and that elderly informants would have heard about
so disturbing an event as a defiant homicide anywhere among the Siriono.
    i. For the Tupinamba, the homicide data is seventeenth century, the population estimate
sixteenth century.
    j. I have followed Morgan on the Iroquois, but with skepticism: Fenton's case records
of suicide incidentally mention three homicides among the Seneca.
    k. For Laos, the homicide data are *ca.* 1935, the population estimate *ca.* 1953.

exact or that all homicides there reported are defiant homicides; I do say they constitute persuasive evidence that some
peoples have homicide rates well above 5 per 100,000.

    Veniaminov [14] in over ten years of residence learned of
no cases of homicide at all among the Aleut; Linton's [15] informants among the Tanala (whose population is 200,000 in

all) knew of no recent cases; and Hudspeth [16] knew of only one recent homicide among the Miao (who number about 150,000 in all). A true frequency of one homicide or less in 40 years would be plausible evidence of a low rate among the Aleut, of four or less in one year among the Tanala, or three or less in one year among the Miao.

Returning to the UN statistics, again I cite only the most trustworthy reports—those from countries claiming at least 90 per cent complete reports and classifying not more than 10 per cent of all deaths in the category including unknown causes. A number of Western European countries with general reputations for efficient police and careful statistics report extremely low homicide rates: Netherlands reports only 3 per million; Ireland, Northern Ireland, and Norway only 4 per million; Denmark only 5 per million. It is necessary to suppose that the true rate is at least *ten times* as great as that reported in order to doubt that these countries have low rates. In all, 18 of these countries report rates less than one-half as great as the base rate of 5 per 100,000.[17] It is hard for me to suppose that in all these countries the police fail to record half of the homicides that occur—especially since by definition I have excluded homicides disguised so as to be mistaken for natural or accidental death.

I have shown that homicide rates are high among some people and low among other people. Considerable variance exists, and there is no doubt that true variance is one of the factors producing the variance in reports of Table 13. How plausible is the suspicion that Table 14 also reflects my bias as comparativist or bias of informants or ethnographers?

Bias in Comparativist's Inferences

Table 14 presents the homicide data from which come the arrays of *high* and *low* incidence of defiant homicide in Table 1. Since there may be doubt that ethnographers take into consideration the number of people involved when reporting in vague terms the frequency of homicides, I have distinguished small populations (under 10,000) from large ones, feeling greater confidence in high reports from small populations and low reports from large populations. The columns of Table 14: (1) name the people reported and specify the period of time involved; (2) give the OQI (observation quality index); (3) cite the source of the report; (4) state the reported rate; (5) give the incidence report for the nine "rate reported" people; (6) show the plausible incidence for an individual inference of high (low) rate after considering extrapolation and population estimate error (as already explained in detail above); and (7) state the estimated mean population during the period in question. Incidence and rate reports for peoples under 50,000 population cover living memory periods (40 years for *low* rates, 80 years for *high* rates, as explained above in the discussion of extrapolation error); for peoples over 50,000 population, incidence and rate reports are for one year.

The bias in the present study which I have as the comparativist is toward showing a variance; it is in my interest that rates which seem low actually be low, that rates which seem high actually be high. I am tempted to believe my sources and must discipline myself to be critical. Let us see what effect my bias can have had on the classifications of defiant homicide.

I class as *high* rates those of above 5 per 100,000 people per year (5 per 2,000 people per 50-year period); as *low*, rates below that. Eight reports can be put in rate form, either as specified rates or as inequalities, and classified on that basis. Nine other reports can be classified as high or low simply on the basis of statements in the sources implying or strongly suggesting such a classification, even though nothing further can be said about rates.

Fourteen reports are unclassifiable: 2 report an incidence under 9 per 100,000; and 12 report the presence of defiant homicide with no indication of rate.

On only 4 of the 17 classifications is my subjective judgment a deciding factor. (On one other, I use it to make an inference on the rate, but the report is emphatically low.) On 12 of the 16, the ethnographers unequivocally assert a high (2) or low (10) rate.

Seven of the eight rate reports reflect counts by ethnographers. B. Whiting [18] gives case histories of five homicides among the Northern Paiute and reports that still others also took place. Ray [19] cites a Southeast Salish informant who remembered "six murders" in his lifetime. Van Valkenburgh [20] says that there were "not . . . over five murders on the Navaho Reservation" in 1936; Hudspeth [21] knows of only one recent homicide among the Miao. Informants flatly denied any knowledge of homicides in living memory among the Toda, the Aleut and the Tanala. (Similar denials were made among the Timbira and the Ifalik, but since these tribes number less than 400 each, these denials do not report a rate below 5 per 2,000).

Holmberg [22] says homicide is "almost unknown" among the Siriono (I have treated this remark as evidence of one case in living memory). Stout [23] says "murder is rare" among the Cuna. Dorsey [24] says that for a time among the Omaha, "drunkenness . . . often led to murder." Landes [25] say cautiously that "outright murder does not appear to be common" among the Ojibwa; true, against this Kinietz [26] mentions "at least two homicides in recent years" by drunken people but a frequency of 45 or fewer homicides in 80 years would constitute plausible evidence of a low rate among the 30,000 Ojibwa.

Morgan [27] says that "crime" is "infrequent" among the

Iroquois (but Fenton [28] in the course of his suicide study mentions three cases of homicide). According to Thompson, [29] "crimes" are "few" in Laos.

All four subjective inferences of mine involve high rates. Institutionalized secret ritual murder by specialist murderers is described among the Khasi and the Tiv (no evidence suggests that these murders are approved or condoned by the kin of the slayers; see Rules 2.2 and 2.3); while ethnographers make no statements about frequency, they describe the practice in considerable detail as a regular part of the Khasi and Tiv ways of life. Among the Tupinamba, Heriarte [30] reports many drunken brawls, "some of which result in death"; Cardim [31] supports him by noting that "headbreaking" takes place at Tupinamba feasts. Among the Copper Eskimo, both Rasmussen [32] and Jenness [33] discuss homicides in some detail, leaving a distinct impression that they are common—eight or more homicides in living memory would constitute plausible evidence of a high rate among the Copper Eskimo.

Statistical Quality Control Tests

None of the tests for bias in defiant homicide reports proved statistically significant. However, since only 19 societies yielded data adequate for testing and several Q coefficients were rather high, the work leaves us apprehensive about the presence of bias in the minds of ethnographer and comparativist although it is more reassuring about the absence of bias in the minds of informants. The absence of any important bias in the minds of informants is indicated by Tests 1 and 2: Test 1 failed to show any significant relationship between the collection of specific case frequency data by the ethnographer and high defiant homicide reports ($Q = 0.35$); Test 2 failed to show any relationship at all between the use of participant-observation field methods and high defiant homicide reports ($Q = 0.00$). Tests 3 and 4 suggest the possibility of bias in the ethnographer's mind: There may be a relationship between high defiant homicide reports and ethnographer's length of stay in the field ($Q = 0.66$); there may also be a relationship between high defiant homicide reports and ethnographer's familiarity with the native language ($Q = 0.71$); true, neither of these coefficients attains statistical significance but they are high enough for us to fear that a larger sample might well do so. On the other hand, Test 5 fails to provide any support at all for the hypothesis that high defiant homicide reports are related to ethnographer's role (professional social scientist or native scholar treated as "favorable" roles; others as "unfavorable") $Q = 0.00$. Test 6 strongly suggests the possibility that I as comparativist have consistently tended to classify vague or ungeneralized defiant homicide reports as high ($Q = -0.80$); the relationship just misses being statistically significant at the 5 per cent level. Test 7 does not provide support for the hypothesis of a cumulative bias involving the first two stages of the ethnological research process; the relationship between high defiant homicide reports and the observation quality index (OQI) apparently is less than that found in the case of either of the two most threatening sources of bias in ethnographer's mind ($Q = 0.52$). Since there were only four societies with more than one independent defiant homicide report, we have no adequate indication of the extent of random error in these reports: of these four societies, three sets of reports were in agreement, the fourth set concerning the Iroquois may or may not constitute a case of disagreement—it is discussed further in the following section. To sum up, the study has given no reason to fear bias in informant's mind on frequency of defiant homicide but has indicated some grounds for concern about bias in ethnographer's mind and even more grounds for concern about bias in the comparativist's mind. Studies involving tests of correlational hypotheses which make use of ethnographic data on homicide clearly need to use data quality control to test for bias in this indicator and its hypothetical correlates; if both variables prove to have a reporting bias, some sort of control for spurious correlation will become essential.

CONTROL OF THE PROTEST SUICIDE INDICATOR

Table 15 shows the data on protest suicide. I have no thought of accurately stating exact rates of protest suicide from existing reports. I seek only to distinguish high rates from low. I do not feel very confident that every single one of the peoples attributed a high suicide rate in Table 1 has in fact a higher rate than every one of the peoples attributed a low rate. But I now show reasons for my confidence that most of the peoples in the *high* array have higher rates than most of the people in the *low* array. I begin by reviewing the evidence that substantial differences in suicide rates do exist among various cultures, primitive and civilized —in other words, that there is a variance. Next I explain the reasoning behind the entries in the tables; here I give special attention to the possibility of bias in my inferences as comparativist. Finally, I use the individual indicators and the composite OQI to test the field reports for evidence of bias among informants or ethnographers. Again I say: systematic bias is the main problem in data quality control here. If correlations of these arrays with others prove significant, evidence of random error only goes to indicate that the true correlations are even higher.

Table 15—Protest Suicide Reports

People	OQI	Reporter	RR	IR	PI	Population
		RATE REPORTS				
Paiute (Harney Valley), 1856–1935	3	Whiting 1950:70f	117	23	6	245
Vietnamese (Hanoi City), 1927–1936	4	# Vu Cong Hoe 1937:4,6	19.5	24.2	21	124,000
Iroquois (Seneca), 1855–1936	2	# Fenton 1941	6.48	11	7	2,870
Toda, 1822–1901	1	# Rivers 1906:555	6.12	3	1	610
Navaho (San Juan County), 1900–1942	2	# Wyman and Thorne 1945:278f	5.15	10	16	4,630
Apayao, 1899–1938	3	# Vanoverbergh 1936–1938:238	<1	1	31	**11,000**
Tanala, ca. 1927	2	# Linton 1933:313	<1	0	12	200,000
Azande, annual rate 1921–1932	2	# Larken 1926–1927:17	<1	"rare"	172	2,000,000
Ifalik, 1909–1948	2	# Spiro 1950:203	<10	0	ab-sent	304
		VAGUE REPORTS				

Rate Seems High—Population Below 10,000

People	OQI	Reporter	RR	IR	PI	Population
Aleut, 1756–1835	3	# Veniaminov 1840a:28f,32f; # Veniaminov 1840b:8f; (# Coxe 1804:258f)			61	2,580
Southeast Salish (Sanpoil), 1851–1930	2	# Ray 1933:149			9	486
Tikopia, 1851–1930	7	# Firth 1931:514f; # Firth 1930: 90; # Firth 1949:180; # Firth 1951: 168; # Rivers 1914:347; P. Dillon in Wisse 1933:20			18	1,281
Pukapuka, 1856–1935	4	# Beaglehole 1938:373 # Beaglehole, n.d.:53f			9	478

Table 15—Protest Suicide Reports (Cont.)

Rate Seems High—Population Over 10,000

Tupinamba, 1500–1580	2	# Soares de Souza 1851:323; (# Magalhaes de Gandova 1922:173	367	**39,000**
Jivaro, 1868– 1928	1	# Brüning 1928:50; (# Rivet 1907:239; # Tessmann 1930: 362; Karsten 1935:223)	185	**20,000**
Mbundu, date uncertain	0	Tucker in # Hambly 1934:125	?	?
Koreans, ca. 1909	4	# Moose 1911:110f; # Griffis 1882: 255; (# Bergman 1938:54)	1,768	16,900,000
Miao, ca. 1937	4	# Graham 1937:40; # Hudspeth 1937:43f	24	150,000
Rwala, 1828– 1908	3	# Musil 1928:240	313	**35,000**

Rate Seems Low—Population Over 10,000

Cambodia, ca. 1924	0	# Franck 1926:81f; Thompson 1937:325)	182	2,100,000

Rate Seems Low—Population Below 10,000

Copper Eskimo, 1876–1916	0	# Jenness 1922:233; but see # Rasmussen 1932:46f	absent	304

UNCLASSIFIABLE REPORTS

Report Seems Greater than 3 per 100,000

Omaha, 1835– 1905	4	# Fletcher and LaFleche 1911: 132, 588	1,215
Ojibwa, 1895— 1935	3	Keating in Wisse 1933:159; Ruth Landes, private communication	30,000
Timbira, 1833– 1933	3	# Nimuendaju 1946:108, 123,133	**299**

Protest Suicide Occurs—No Suggestion of Rate

Aranda, Apayao, Ashanti, Azande, Carib, Chagga, Ifugao, Koreans, Mbundu, Pukapuka, Rwala, Samoa.

Comments: See Table 14 for explanation of captions and entries. The incidence reports on the Seneca and the San Juan County Navaho are considered incomplete by their authors. The vast majority of suicides are women among the Jivaro, Koreans, Miao, Rwala, and Ojibwa; suicide is apparently rather uncommon among men of these groups. The Toda computation is based on 80 years, because explicitly reported as covering four generations.

No standard error of the mean of population estimate was computed for the Seneca or the Toda since only one pair was available; the Toda and Pukapuka estimates of population at the middle point of the period were derived by extrapolation entirely from late estimates, though in both instances extrapolation covered only about a decade.

Existence of Variance

There is formidable evidence that suicide rates do often differ greatly. The present modest sample offers strongly contrasting reports. On one hand, B. Whiting [34] in genealogies counted 23 suicides among about 250 Paiute. After allowing for extrapolation error and error in population estimate, as many as 6 suicides would be a plausible high incidence. There cannot be the slightest doubt that the Harney Valley Paiute had a very high suicide rate during the period 1856–1935. On the other hand, there are some 200,000 Tanala, yet Linton's [35] informants could not recall a single suicide—a maximum of 12 suicides in one year constitutes plausible evidence that the Tanala rate is low. Larken [36] served as an official among the Azande for over twenty years; he reports that suicide is rare among them; a true frequency of 172 or fewer suicides in one year constitutes plausible evidence that the Azande rate is low.

From other peoples not in this sample, there is much more evidence. By the nature of things, it is easier to authenticate a high rate than a low one; for once it is established that the Paiute have had more than 6 suicides in 50 years we are unconcerned how many others may have been overlooked by informants or field workers. The statistical bureaus of Austria, Denmark, West Berlin and Switzerland all report suicide rates above *20* per 100,000 per year.[37] Wisse's survey of primitive suicide has as one of its chief conclusions the verification of the Steinmetz hypothesis that suicide is frequent among many primitive peoples. Wisse [38] lists 56 out of 377 peoples in his first or highest frequency class of suicide. His text reviews the evidence in great detail and since he treated his data with reserve and skepticism it seems likely that most if not all these 56 peoples had high suicide rates.

Some low rates seem equally well established. The latest statistics show seven countries reporting suicide rates under 5 per 100,000: Union of South Africa (colored people), Barbados, Canal Zone, Taiwan, Gibraltar, Ireland and Northern Ireland.[39]

Although always skeptical of low suicide reports, Wisse cites several impressive ones. (I have checked all of them myself.) Perhaps the most impressive report is that on the Ona of Tierra del Fuego, who numbered between 2,000 and 4,000 until the end of the nineteenth century.[40] The Ona were often visited over a period of several centuries; the extensive literature on them was thoroughly combed by Cooper [41] and Gusinde—furthermore, Gusinde with these data before him spent several seasons in the field working with surviving Ona informants. Gusinde, one of the most thorough of ethnographers, says flatly: "That suicide was ever committed in Tierra del Fuego is hardly probable. . . . My informants knew nothing about suicide and my questions confused them so strange a concept did it seem to them." [42] Cooper [43] flatly denies the existence of suicide among both Ona and Yaghan. Hrdlicka [44] could learn of no recent case of suicide among the Mohave, Yuma, or Zuni (population then respectively about 2,000, 1,400, and 1,500). According to Scott Robertson, who lived among the Kafirs of the Hindu Kush about a year as an ethnologist, "The idea of a man killing himself strikes them as inexplicable." [45] (Bacon [46] estimates the Kafirs' population at 60,000.) Least prepossessing at first glance is the report on the Kirgis of the Saissank district by Tronoff, as abstracted by Von Stenin.[47] Tronoff seems to have had poor rapport, speaking of these people and their culture with undisguised contempt. Yet, after reporting a high frequency among them of theft, mayhem, and homicide, the report remarks: "Suicide occurs very rarely *(höchst selten)* and then usually because of domestic strife; the Kirgis consider a suicide as a great sin and therefore we need not wonder that the Mullah in the Saissank district refused to give a suicide the last rites or to speak the customary prayers at her grave. She was buried apart from the others at his direction." [48] A census less than a decade earlier returned 53,965 Kirgis in the Saissank district; hence a true frequency of 2 or fewer suicides in one year or 37 or less in one decade would constitute plausible evidence of a low rate.

Voegelin [49] studied suicide among several tribes of northeastern California, reporting low rates from practically all of them. No suicides at all either recent or aboriginal could be called to mind by informants among the Shasta, the Hayfork Wintu, or the Maidu (except Nisenan [50]), only one case each among the Modoc [51] and the Nisenan,[52] and only two cases each among the Atsugewi [53] and the Surprise Valley Paiute.[54]

Bias in Comparativist's Inferences

Table 15 presents the suicide data from which came the arrays of *high* and *low* incidence of protest suicide in Table 1. I class as *high* rates those above 10 per 100,000 people per year (10 per 2,000 people per 50-year period); as *low,* rates below that. Nine reports can be put in rate form, either as specific rates or as inequalities, and classified *high* or *low* on that basis. Fifteen other reports contain statements (analyzed below) implying or suggesting a *high* or *low* rate. Three reports (Omaha, Ojibwa, Timbira) can be classed as apparently reflecting a rate greater than 3 (per 100,000 per year) but cannot be classified *high* or *low.*

The rate reports are of four types. The Paiute and Toda reports reflect suicide data from genealogies as compiled by

B. Whiting [55] and Rivers.[56] The Vietnamese report reflects Hanoi city vital statistics records compiled by Vu Cong Hoe.[57] The Iroquois and Navaho reports are special monographs on suicides whose authors worked months seeking full lists. I tabulate all the suicides since 1855 Fenton [58] could learn about among the Seneca and all the suicides since 1900 that Wyman and Thorne [59] could learn about among the San Juan County Navaho (neither report claims to be complete). Among the Apayao, Vanoverbergh's [60] informants knew of only one suicide, and Linton's [61] informants among the Tanala knew of none at all; since there are 11,000 Apayao and 200,000 Tanala I have tabulated these reports as indicating a rate of less than 1 per 100,000 per year. Larken [62] speaking of the Azande simply says that suicide is rare among them, but, since there are so many Azande (about two million) and since Larken was among them so long, I have likewise taken this as a report of a rate under 1 per 100,000 per year; I assume that if Larken had been aware of as many as 20 suicides a year among the Azande he would not have said suicide is rare among them. My inference then about these rate reports is that the best information available to their authors indicates a high rate among the Paiute and Vietnamese and a low rate among the others. I make no inferences about the confidence that these authors feel about their information. By reducing the information reported to rate terms, I have substantially eliminated the risk that I distort what the ethnographers report they have learned about suicide among the people they have studied. The trustworthiness of the reports themselves is of course a matter for data quality control.

Nine of the vague reports involve no rate inferences by the comparativist. In three of these nine, the ethnographer himself generalizes about suicide rates, and I take his word for it. Graham [63] says "a great many" Ch'uan Miao women commit suicide, that suicide "seems almost fashionable" among them; and Hudspeth [64] says the Miao have a "tendency readily to commit suicide." Tucker [65] says suicide is "common" among the Mbundu. Franck [66] says suicide is "rare" among the Cambodians, and Thompson [67] says it is "very rare" among them.

In the other six reports, the ethnographer does not generalize about suicide rates but does mention a general set of circumstances in which a specified category of person commits suicide, without indicating how often circumstances of this sort occur. In three of these six reports (Koreans, Pukapuka, Tupinamba) it seems clear to me from the cultural context that the circumstances occur often; in the other three (Southeast Salish, Jivaro, Rwala) I am not so sure. Among the Koreans, Moose [68] says that young wives unhappy at the treatment by their mothers-in-law (who dominate the patrilocal extended family households) "often" commit suicide, and Griffis [69] says that young widows (who occupy a peculiarly difficult position) "often" do so too. Among the Pukapuka, the Beagleholes [70] report that in general a person thoroughly shamed will commit suicide, and they give examples. Soares de Souza [71] says of the Tupinamba that "when they get upset" they kill themselves.

Among the Southeast Salish, Ray [72] says that when eloping couples were apprehended, it was "not uncommon" for the girl to commit suicide; forced marriage "sometimes" also resulted in the suicide of the bride. Tessmann [73] says that Jivaro women suicide when they are forced to live with a man who may treat them badly, or for whom they do not care, a generalization supported by comments in Karsten,[74] Rivet,[75] and Brüning.[76] Among the Rwala, pregnant unmarried girls "often" commit suicide, according to Musil.[77]

(When such a girl's condition becomes known, her father or brothers probably will kill her if they can. These suicides then could be conceivably thought of as suicides to avoid execution for a capital offense and hence, by definition, as involuntary suicides rather than protest suicides. On the other hand, a girl in trouble would have several months to run away if she wished, a difficult and harsh but not impossible course. On balance, I class these Rwala deaths as protest suicides.)

In one report, the Copper Eskimo, Jenness [78] flatly says that suicide is extremely rare, that he only knows of one case, while Rasmussen [79] without asserting that he knows of any specific cases, describes a number of circumstances in which suicide occurs. I follow the man with the higher OQI. (Privately, I find two hypotheses plausible to explain the conflict: (1) Jenness [80] may not have inquired diligently into suicide but simply recorded what happened to come to mind; (2) Rasmussen,[81] who also worked with a number of other Eskimo groups, may have mixed up other Eskimo data with his Copper Eskimo report.)

This leaves only two vague reports on which I could not avoid using judgment about frequency to make a decision. These are inferences readily subject to my bias, and I have marked both with question marks in the Incidence Report column.

1. Veniaminov [82] says suicide is uncommon among the Aleut but produces a wealth of data to show that on the contrary it is very common indeed; he supports his own conclusion at one point by arguing that a person who suicides from grief at the death of a loved one cannot be classed as a suicide at all: "Otherwise any sacrifice performed out of love for another person may be given that name." [83] To understand Veniaminov's attitude, one must remember that

he is a priest who has had no training in tolerance for other customs and considers suicide a hideous sin but at the same time has a warm feeling for his Aleuts and their culture. What he really means to say, I think, is what every anthropologist today would say as a matter of course: we should not morally judge Aleut suicide by orthodox Christian standards. Wisse [84] concludes his review of the literature on Aleut suicide by classing all the Aleut (with the probable exception of the Fox Island people) as having very high suicide rates.

2. All the writers on the Tikopia report high frequencies of suicide there, but the circumstances described by Firth [85] seem to involve involuntary suicides very often. My guess is that at least six protest suicides take place in 50 years among the Tikopia, and at least as many more involuntary suicides.

Statistical Quality Control Tests

Considerable indication of varied types of biases in protest suicide reports is provided by this study. The equivalence of our case report rate defintion of high suicide rate and the impressionistic qualitative reports of ethnographers is brought into question by our first two tests, whose contradictory results otherwise would lack any plausible explanation except a freak sample: Test 1 has a high and almost statistically significant Q coefficient (-0.89) indicating a tendency for quantitative reports to be less likely to report high suicide rates than qualitative reports. On the other hand, reports based on participant observation field methods seem to be more likely to report high suicide rates than those not so based ($Q = 0.78$). It is hoped that more light will be thrown on this seeming contradiction by further research on a new sample being conducted by the writer.

Bias in ethnographers' minds is suggested by only one of our three tests for it: Test 3 shows no significant relationship between high protest suicide reports and ethnographer's length of stay in field ($Q = 0.29$); Test 5 shows no relationship at all between high suicide reports and ethnographer's role ($Q = 0.00$); but Test 4 shows a high and nearly significant relationship between high suicide reports and ethnographer's native language familiarity ($Q = 0.88$).

Furthermore, there is solid support for the existence of a consistent bias in comparativist's classification of vague or ungeneralized reports; Test 6 shows a high negative coefficient ($Q = -0.89$), statistically significant at the 1 per cent level.

Finally, Test 7 shows a high and nearly significant relationship between the observation quality index and high suicide reports ($Q = 0.83$). All in all, these tests for bias show that the classification methods used in this exploratory study are unsatisfactory and need to be revised.

Concerning random error, we have six societies on which more than one independent report was made. Five of these sets of reports agreed; the sixth conflicted.

CONTROL OF THE WITCHCRAFT ATTRIBUTION INDICATOR

The quality control tests of witchcraft attribution reports are in many ways the most interesting of all. The tests of bias in field reports produce statistically significant evidence of bias; and further strongly suggest that professional anthropologists are not as accurate reporters of witchcraft attribution frequency as missionaries or government officials. The review of possible bias in comparativist's inferences casts grave doubt on the reliability of impressionistic classifications of the importance of witchcraft attribution from vague reports—and hence by implication impeaches the conclusions of two leading cross-cultural surveys. Table 16 presents the witchcraft attribution data.

Table 16—Frequency of Witchcraft Attribution

People	OQI	Reporter
GROUP I: MOST SUPERNATURAL EXPLANATIONS OF DEATH INVOLVE WITCHCRAFT		
Navaho, 1930's	8	#Kluckhohn 1944:15,16,18,31; #Van Valkenburgh 1936:51
Jivaro, 1916–1928	4	#Karsten 1935:269f
Thonga, 1895–1909	3	#Junod 1927:319
Azande, ca. 1930	4	#Evans-Pritchard 1937:479
Tiv, 1916–1936	4	#East 1939:91, 235f
Miao, ca. 1900	3	Hudspeth 1937:24-26
Aranda, ca. 1900	3	Spencer & Gillen in Coon 1948:230
GROUP II: WITCHCRAFT EXPLANATIONS COMMON BUT PROPORTION UNCERTAIN		

IIa. Witchcraft Seems of Major Importance in Culture:

People	OQI	Reporter
Northern Paiute, 1936–8	3	#Whiting 1950:28,33,60
Ojibwa, 1932–1935	2	#Landes 1937:18,132-4
Tupinamba, ca. 1580	4	#Soares de Souza 1851:322; #Evreux 1864:313,340-344
Carib (Barama River), ca. 1932	2	#Gillin 1936:77f, 144-151,159,186
Mbundu, 1933–1938	3	#Childs 1949:58
Ifugao, 1908–1914	4	#Barton 1919:69-72

IIb. Witchcraft Seems of Minor Importance in Culture:

People	OQI	Reporter
Copper Eskimo, 1913–1916	4	#Jenness 1922:95
Southeast Salish, ca. 1929	4	#Ray 1933:206,208; #Teit 1930:196
Omaha, ca. 1905	7	#Fletcher and LaFleche 1911:583,602 #Fortune 1932:86f; #Marshall 1950:197
Chagga, 1906–1926	2	#Raum 1940:369
Ashanti, ca. 1921	3	#Rattray 1939:313
Koreans, ca. 1950	1	#Turner 1950:2f
Cambodia, ca. 1930	1	#Porée and Maspero 1938:8, 201
Vietnam, 1927–1935	2	#Gourou 1945:453
Toda, ca. 1901	1	#Rivers 1906:555
Rwala, ca. 1909	3	#Musil 1928:401f, 408
Tikopia, ca. 1930	4	#Firth 1939:114
GROUP III: MOST SUPERNATURAL EXPLANATIONS OF DEATH INVOLVE SPIRITS		
Aleut, ca. 1790	0	#Sarytschew 1806:76
Siriono, ca. 1941	2	#Holmberg 1950:86
Tanala, ca. 1926	2	#Linton 1933:226
Khasi, ca. 1910	3	#Stegmiller 1921:10, 13
Apayao, ca. 1937	3	#Vanoverbergh 1936–1938:237–39
Ifalik, ca. 1947	7	#Burrows 1949:197; #Spiro 1949:60.
Pukapuka, ca. 1934	4	#Beaglehole and Beaglehole 1936:332

See Table 14 for Explanation of Captions and Entries.

Statistical Quality Control Tests

Just as the protest suicide statistical quality control tests cast doubt on the soundness of our protest suicide indicator design, so the witchcraft attribution statistical quality control tests cast doubt on the validity of one of their number— Test 5, involving ethnographer's role. Furthermore, the tests definitely establish the existence of a bias in the ethnographers' minds—a bias presumably reflecting deliberate and consistent deception of ethnographers by informants.

Since witchcraft attribution is defined as a belief of the informants, informants' bias is excluded by definition. Hence, the use of participant-observation by ethnographers is presumably irrelevant and we would expect no relationship between this use and witchcraft attribution reports; Test 2 produces a Q coefficient of approximately 0.50 that presumably reflects mere chance association.

The existence of bias in the ethnographers' minds, presumably reflecting systematic deliberate deception by informants, is shown by Tests 3 and 4. Test 3 shows high association between length of field stay by ethnographers and high witchcraft attribution reports ($Q = 0.86$, significant at 5 per cent level). Test 4 shows a high association between native language familiarity and high witchcraft attribution reports ($Q = 0.88$; just falls short of statistical significance). These results support the theory of data quality control, presumably reflecting the fact that ethnographers who stay longer in the field or who master the native language have better rapport with informants and hence are less likely to be imposed upon or more likely to detect imposition when imposition is tried.

The result of the third test of bias in ethnographer's mind has interesting implications of another sort, as has already been pointed out in Chapter 4. The occurrence of negative association ($Q = -0.57$) between supposedly "favorable" field roles and high witchcraft attribution reports was there shown to be apparently a reflection of the fact that anthropologists are less likely than missionaries to spend a long time in the field or to learn the native language.

Test 6 is reassuring about the importance of bias in the comparativist's mind in influencing classification of vague or ungeneralized witchcraft attribution reports; there is no indication of a consistent bias here ($Q = 0.22$).

Test 7 is of comparatively little value to us here since it reflects the contrary influences of Control Factors 3 and 4 on one hand and of Control Factor 5 on the other; presumably for this reason the coefficient is neither high nor near statistical significance ($Q = 0.50$).

Finally, the information about random error in the whole process presents no grounds for alarm: all five of the societies on which more than one independent witchcraft attribution report was made presented sets of reports in agreement with each other.

While witchcraft is a difficult topic for the field worker to study in many ways, the greatest danger of ethnographer's bias seems to arise from the possibility that he may believe denials by informants of any knowledge of witchcraft, when, in fact, witchcraft attribution is common but informants are afraid to talk for fear of retaliation by witches or of being thought witches themselves, or from a general sense of embarrassment about the whole subject. The discussion of the field worker's problem among the Navaho by Kluckhohn [86] is especially enlightening. Kluckhohn's analysis is borne out by Ralph Beals, who, in discussing this topic at an anthropological meeting, remarked that among the Indians of Mexico where he has worked, the more important witchcraft attribution is to the people, the more likely informants are to deny its existence entirely.

To sum up, these tests have not turned up any reason for concern about informants' bias, comparativists' bias or random error; but they definitely show the existence of ethnographers' bias. This showing makes the use of data quality control essential in any correlational studies involving witchcraft attribution, and where a like bias is revealed for any of the traits apparently correlated with this one, control for spurious correlation reflecting reporting bias is essential. For this reason, I must express lack of confidence in the conclusion of Beatrice Whiting that a high development of belief in witchcraft is associated with a lack of formal government,[87] and must also express lack of confidence in the conclusion of Whiting and Child that a high development of a belief in witchcraft is associated with certain child-training practices.[88] Both of these conclusions require data quality control to confirm or correct the hypothesis that the observed correlations merely reflect biases in the ethnological research process.

Bias in Comparativist's Inferences

In 14 of the classifications (Table 16: Groups I and III) no subjective judgments of mine as comparativist were involved. The remaining 17 classifications (Group II) depend upon my impression of the general importance of witchcraft attribution in the culture; the reliability of these 17 classifications has been tested and discredited. Among the 17 peoples of Group II, witchcraft attribution is reported present; but it is not possible to say what proportion of supernatural deaths are thus explained. Of this group, 6 people are put into Subgroup IIa: among them witchcraft attribution seemed to me to play a part of major importance in the culture; the remaining 11 are put into Subgroup IIb: among them witchcraft attribution seemed to me of minor importance in the culture. Since this classification of the Group II peoples into subgroups is a subjective judgment, it is well to compare it with the like judgments of others. The comparison is not encouraging: of these 17 borderline cases, a total of 16 comparisons could be made with either the rating of B. Whiting or of the judges of Whiting and Child; seven ratings agreed, nine disagreed—about what we would expect from sheer chance.

This finding does not conflict with the report of higher reliability of judgments of importance of sorcery by B. Whiting [89] or by Whiting and Child [90]: both these studies included clear cases like my Groups I and III as well as borderline cases like my Group II. Perhaps a more reliable procedure in future studies might be to classify Group II societies into those among which at least one execution for witchcraft has occurred in living memory and those in which none has. This would make the witchcraft attribution criterion relevant to societies that either attribute a majority of deaths to witchcraft whether or not they execute for it, or that have executed for alleged witchcraft whether or not they attribute a majority of supernatural deaths to it. Such a twofold criterion would reduce the need for uncertain subjective classifications.

CHAPTER 8

Conclusion

               This study resulted from a search for traits which might be useful in cross-cultural surveys of culture stress. The search was focused on traits which were intuitively felt to be symptoms of culture stress and the problem emphasized was that of discovering traits which were adequately reported in existing ethnographic literature as compiled in the Human Relations Area Files. On five traits, there proved to be insufficient data in the Files for use; if the Files are indeed representative samples of ethnographic literature, the following traits cannot be effectively studied in a library cross-cultural survey but demand much further field work: (1) use of narcotics, (2) personality disorders, (3) offenses against the mores other than homicide, (4) psychosomatic illnesses, and (5) stuttering. On the other hand, considerable data were found on four traits, whose analysis became the focus of the study: (1) suicide, (2) homicide, (3) alcohol use, and (4) belief in sorcery. From these traits, a tentative index of culture stress is proposed, involving four carefully defined concepts: (1) drunken brawling,

(2) defiant homicide, (3) protest suicide, and (4) witchcraft attribution.

The reports on these traits were not based on field work of such rigor and completeness that reporting error could be ignored. On the contrary, reporting error might well be presumed to influence the reports greatly. Hence, before these reports could be offered for use in a cross-cultural survey of culture stress, a means of detecting and controlling reporting error had to be devised. For that purpose the method of data quality control is here presented.

The data quality control tests indicated that drunken brawling reports were not subject to any important reporting bias, either on the part of the informants, the ethnographers or the comparativist; drunken brawling reports can be considered in working control and correlations derived from their use can be accepted as reflecting real associations in the behavior of the people studied rather than mere reflections of distortions in the data collection process. The data quality control tests for defiant homicide failed to produce significant evidence of reporting bias; however Control Factors 3, 4, and 6 produced fairly high coefficients of association approaching statistical significance. Since the sample studied was comparatively small, it seems well warranted to conclude that future cross-cultural surveys using homicide as a trait ought to test for these three control factors in order to avoid the risk of spurious correlation reflecting mere distortions in the data collection process. The data quality control tests for protest suicide produced significant evidence of reporting bias with control Factor 6, as well as high though not quite significant evidence of reporting bias with Control Factor 4; thus future cross-cultural surveys using suicide as a trait clearly must test for Factor 6 and evidently ought also to test for Factor 4 in order to avoid the risk of spurious correlation. Furthermore, the high and contradictory results of

Factors 1 and 2 suggest that the element of concept definition equating rate reports with qualitative reports may be invalid, and thus suggest the desirability of revising the concept definition of protest suicide or, alternatively, discarding one of the two control factors. Further research on this problem is clearly needed. Finally, the data quality control tests for witchcraft attribution produced statistically significant evidence of second stage bias in witchcraft attribution reports. This indicates that the use of data quality control is mandatory in cross-cultural surveys using sorcery data, and raises doubts about the findings of two earlier such studies.

These then are the findings on symptoms of culture stress. These findings also constitute the first test of data quality control as a research tool. Their failure to turn up any evidence of bias on drunken brawling reports constitutes a demonstration that drunken brawling reports collected under circumstances generally considered disadvantageous may be used as safely as those collected under circumstances generally considered advantageous and hence gives us strong support for any correlations later derived between drunken brawling and any other traits; logically, one is compelled to choose between two conclusions; either there is no significant bias in drunken brawling reports or else drunken brawling reports collected by better field techniques are about as badly biased as those collected by worse ones. I submit therefore that the drunken brawling control tests not only show the trustworthiness of the drunken brawling reports but the usefulness of data quality control.

This usefulness is further demonstrated by the statistically significant evidence of reporting bias in protest suicide and witchcraft attribution reports. Even with a sample this small and statistical formulas this insensitive, data quality control has proved its ability to discriminate between trustworthy and untrustworthy trait report sets. However, the uncer-

162

9. F. W. Walbank, *Aratos of Sicyon* (London: Cambridge University Press, 1933).

10. Wilhelm Schmidt, *The Culture Historical Method of Ethnology,* translated by S. A. Sieber (New York: Fortuny's, 1937–1939).

11. John M. Cooper, *An Analytical and Critical Bibliography of the Tierra del Fuego and Adjacent Territory,* Bureau of American Ethnology, Bulletin No. 63 (Washington: Government Printing Office, 1917).

12. Martin Gusinde, *Die Feuerland Indianer,* 2 vols. (Mödling bei Wien: Anthropos, 1931 *et seq.*).

13. See Acheson J. Duncan, *Quality Control and Industrial Statistics,* (Homewood, Ill.: Irwin, 1955); also American Standards Association, *Control Chart Method of Controlling Quality during Production,* Pamphlet Z1.3 (New York: American Standards Association, 1942).

14. Raoul Naroll, "A Preliminary Index of Social Development," *American Anthropologist,* LXIII (1956), 692.

15. Harold E. Driver, "An Integration of Functional, Evolutionary and Historical Theory by Means of Correlations," *International Journal of American Linguistics,* Memoir XII (Indiana University Publications in Anthropology and Linguistics, 1956), 1–36.

16. Abraham Wald, *Sequential Analysis* (New York: Wiley, 1947); Statistical Research Group, Columbia University, *Sequential Analysis of Statistical Data: Applications,* rev. ed. (New York: Columbia University Press, 1946).

17. G. U. Yule and M. G. Kendall, *An Introduction to the Theory of Statistics,* 12th ed. (London: Griffin, 1940) on theory of partial association; Paul F. Lazersfeld and Morris Rosenberg, *The Language of Social Research* (New York: Free Press of Glencoe, 1955), section II, on applications of partial association; Margaret J. Hagood and Daniel O. Price, *Statistics for Sociologists,* rev. ed. (New York: Holt, 1952), Part IV, on the other techniques mentioned.

18. U.S. War Department, *The War of Rebellion: Official Records of the Union and Confederate Armies* (Washington: 1880–1901, 128 vols.)

19. Clarence C. Buel and Robert V. Johnson, eds., *Battles and Leaders of the Civil War* (New York: 1887, 4 vols.).

20. See Naroll, "Sheridan and Cedar Creek," *op. cit.,* pp. 153, 157.

21. Bernard Berelson, "Content Analysis," in Gardner Lindzey, ed., *Handbook of Social Psychology* (Reading, Mass.: Addison-Wesley, 1954) I:488–522.

22. Charles A. Beard, "That Noble Dream," *American Historical Review,* XLI (1935) 74–87; Charles A. Beard, "Written History as an Act of Faith," *American Historical Review,* XXXIX (1934) 219–29.

23. Benedetto Croce, *History: Its Theory and Practice,* tr. by Douglas Ainslee (New York: Harcourt Brace, 1921).

24. Albert Pierce, "The Classification of Documents Relative to Source Proximity," paper read at the public Anthropological Conference sponsored by the Southwestern Anthropological Association and the Wenner-Gren Foundation for Anthropological Research at the University of California, Los Angeles, April 25, 1959.

CHAPTER 2

1. Joseph W. Eaton and Robert J. Weil, *Culture and Mental Disorders: A Comparative Study of Hutterites and Other Populations* (New York: Free Press of Glencoe, 1955).

2. American Anthropological Association, Executive Board, "Statement on Human Rights," *American Anthropologist,* XLIX (1947), 539–43.

3. Ruth Benedict, *Patterns of Culture* (New York: Mentor Books, 1946).

4. John J. Honigmann, *Culture and Personality* (New York: Harper, 1954), pp. 404–13; compare Marvin K. Opler, *Culture, Psychiatry and Human Values* (Springfield, Ill.: Charles C Thomas, 1956), pp. 79, 198f, 214; Hans Selye, *The Stress of Life* (New York: McGraw-Hill, 1956); Leo W. Simmons and Harold G. Wolff, *Social Science in Medicine* (New York: Russell Sage Foundation, 1954), 196f; A. Irving Hallowell, "Psychic Stresses and Culture Patterns," *American Journal of Psychiatry,* XCII (May, 1936), 1297; and John Arsenian and Jean M. Arsenian, "Tough and Easy Cultures," *Psychiatry,* II (1948), 377–85.

5. William S. Robinson, "Ecological Correlations and the Behavior of Individuals," *American Sociological Review,* XV (1950), 351–57; and Herbert Menzel "Comment on Robinson's 'Ecological Correlations and the Behavior of Individuals,'" *American Sociological Review,* XV (1950), 674.

6. Karl Popper, *Logik der Forschung: zur Erkenntnistheorie der Modernen Naturwissenschaft* (Vienna: Julius Springer, 1935).

7. George P. Murdock, *Social Structure* (New York: Macmillan, 1949).

8. John W. M. Whiting and Irvin L. Child, *Child Training and Personality* (New Haven: Yale University Press, 1953).

9. Erik Erikson in George P. Murdock and John W. M. Whiting, "Cultural Determination of Parental Attitudes," in *Problems of Infancy and Childhood, Transactions of the Fourth Conference . . .,* Milton J. E. Senn, ed. (New York: Macy Foundation, 1951), pp. 38f.

10. Whiting and Child, *op. cit.*, p. 59.

11. J. F. Kenney and E. S. Keeping, *Mathematics of Statistics, Part Two*, 2nd ed. (Princeton, N.J.: Van Nostrand, 1951), p. 165.

12. *Ibid.*, pp. 235, 257.

13. *Ibid.*, pp. 178, 207.

14. Murdock, *op. cit.*

15. Compare Lincoln E. Moses, "Nonparametric Statistics for Psychological Research," *Psychological Bulletin*, XLIX (1952), 122–43; Richard I. Savage, "Bibliography of Nonparametric Statistics and Related Topics," *Journal of the American Statistical Association*, XLVIII (1953), 844–906; and Frederick Mosteller and Robert R. Bush, "Selected Quantitative Techniques," in *Handbook of Social Psychology*, Vol. I, Gardner Lindzey, ed. (Reading, Mass.: Addison-Wesley, 1954), pp. 289–334.

16. William G. Madow, "Review of 'Introduction to Statistical Reasoning,'" *Journal of the American Statistical Association*, LIII (1958), 208–12.

17. See I. Schapera, "Some Comments on Comparative Method in Social Anthropology," *American Anthropologist*, LV (1953), 353–61; and Andre J. Köbben, "New Ways of Presenting an Old Idea: The Statistical Method in Social Anthropology," *Journal of the Royal Anthropological Institute*, LXXXII (1952), 129–46.

18. George P. Murdock, "World Ethnographic Sample," *American Anthropologist*, LIX (1957), 664f.

19. George P. Murdock, *Outline of World Cultures* (New Haven: Human Relations Area Files, 1954).

20. See Raoul Naroll, "Two Solutions to Galton's Problem," *Philosophy of Science*, Vol. 28, No. 1 (1961) pp. 15–39; Raoul Naroll, "A Preliminary Index of Social Development," *American Anthropologist*, LVIII (1956), 710f; John W. M. Whiting, "The Cross-Cultural Method," in *Handbook of Social Psychology*, Vol. I, Gardner Lindzey, ed. (Reading, Mass.: Addison-Wesley, 1954), p. 528; Köbben, *op. cit.*, p. 132f; Beatrice Whiting, *Paiute Sorcery*, Viking Fund Publications in Anthropology, No. 15 (New York, 1950), p. 88f; Robert H. Lowie, "Evolution in Cultural Anthropology: A Reply to Leslie White," *American Anthropologist*, XLVIII (1946), 226–30; Franz Boas, "Anthropology and Statistics," in *The Social Sciences and Their Interrelations*, W. F. Ogburn and A. Goldenweiser, eds. (Boston: Houghton Mifflin, 1927), pp. 114-21; and Galton in Edward B. Taylor, "On a Method of Investigating the Development of Institutions Applied to the Laws of Marriage and Descent," *Journal of the Royal Anthropological Institute*, XVIII (1889), 272.

21. James G. Frazer, *The Golden Bough*, 12 Vols., 3rd ed. (London: Macmillan, 1911–1915).

22. Benedict, *op. cit.*, pp. 44f.

23. George P. Murdock, "The Common Denominator of Cultures," in *Science of Man in the World Crisis*, Ralph Linton, ed. (New York: Columbia University Press, 1945), pp. 123–42.

24. Ward H. Goodenough, "Residence Rules," *Southwestern Journal of Anthropology*, XII (1956), 37.

25. Honigmann, *op. cit.*, pp. 404–13.

26. Arsenian and Arsenian, *op. cit.*

27. See C. Daryl Forde, *Habitat, Economy and Society* (London: Methuen, 1937).

28. See Melville J. Herskovits, *Economic Anthropology: A Study in Comparative Economics* (New York: Knopf, 1952); Richard Thurnwald, *Economics in Primitive Communities* (Oxford University Press, 1932); and Margaret Mead, ed., *Cooperation and Competition among Primitive Peoples* (New York: McGraw-Hill, 1937).

29. See Harry H. Turney-High, *Primitive Warfare: Its Practice and Concepts* (Columbia, S.C.: University of South Carolina Press, 1949); Maurice R. Davie, *The Evolution of War*, Vol. I (New Haven: Yale University Press, 1929); and Quincy Wright, *A Study of War*, Vol. I (Chicago: University of Chicago Press, 1942), pp. 527, 565.

30. Clellan S. Forde, *A Comparative Study of Human Reproduction*, Yale University Publications in Anthropology, No. 32 (New Haven: Yale University Press, 1945); and Clellan S. Forde and Frank A. Beach, *Patterns of Sexual Behavior* (New York: Harper, 1953).

31. See Frank W. Moore, *Readings in Cross-Cultural Methodology* (New Haven: HRAF Press, 1961), 279–282.

32. Edwin M. Lemert, *Social Pathology* (New York: McGraw-Hill, 1951) pp. 146–50.

33. See Winifred K. Ward, *Stammering: A Contribution to the Study of Its Problems and Treatment* (London: Hamilton, 1941), p. 3; Ernst Schneider, "Über das Stottern," *Beiheft zur Schweizerischen Zeitschrift für Psychologie und ihre Anwendungen*, XXII (Bern and Stuttgart: Huber, 1953), 9f; City of St. Louis, *Sixty-Second Annual Report of the Board of Education of the City of St. Louis, Missouri, for the Year Ending June 30, 1916*, p. 177; and Sara M. Stinchfield, *Speech Disorders* (New York: Harcourt Brace, 1933) pp. 276, 303.

34. Edwin M. Lemert, "Some Indians Who Stutter," *Journal of Speech and Hearing Disorders*, XVIII (1953) 168–74.

35. John C. Snidecor, "Why the Indian Does Not Stutter," *Quarterly Journal of Speech*, XXXIII (1947), 493–95.

36. Adelaide Bullen, "A Cross-Cultural Approach to the Problem of Stuttering," *Child Development*, XVI (1945), 9.

37. Raoul Naroll, field notes.

38. Bullen, *op. cit.*

39. See Schneider, *loc. cit.;* Florence L. Goodenough, *Exceptional Children* (New York: Appleton-Century-Crofts, 1956), pp. 295–97; and James C. Coleman, *Abnormal Psychology and Modern Life* (New York: Scott, Foresman, 1950), p. 374.

CHAPTER 3

1. Edwin M. Lemert, "Alcoholism and the Sociocultural Situation," *Quarterly Journal of Studies on Alcohol,* XVII (1956), 306–17.
2. Charles R. Snyder, "Culture and Sobriety: A Study of Drinking Factors Related to Sobriety among Jews," *Quarterly Journal of Studies on Alcohol,* XVI (1955), 101–77.
3. Lemert, *op. cit.,* p. 313.
4. Donald Horton, "The Functions of Alcohol in Primitive Societies: A Cross-Cultural Survey," *Quarterly Journal of Studies on Alcohol,* IV (1943), 224.
5. *Ibid.,* p. 223.
6. *Ibid.,* p. 224.
7. *Loc. cit.*
8. Robert Bales, "Cultural Differences in Rates of Alcoholism," *Quarterly Journal of Studies on Alcohol,* VI (1946), 480–99.
9. Compare Bales, *op. cit.*
10. H. C. Brearly, *Homicide in the United States* (Chapel Hill, N.C.: University of North Carolina Press, 1932).
11. Andrew F. Henry and James F. Short, Jr., *Suicide and Homicide* (New York: Free Press of Glencoe, 1954).
12. Carlo Levi, *Christ Stopped at Eboli,* translated by Frances Frenaye (New York: Farrar, Strauss, 1950), pp. 138–40.
13. Pierre B. Schneider, *La tentative de suicide: Étude statistique, clinique, psychologique et catamnestique* (Paris and Neuchatel: Delachaux, 1954), pp. 45–59.
14. Don D. Jackson, "Theories of Suicide," in *Clues to Suicide,* Edwin S. Schneidman and N. L. Farberow, eds. (New York: McGraw-Hill, 1957), pp. 11–21.
15. Schneider, *op. cit.,* p. 49.
16. Jakob Wisse, *Selbstmord und Todesfurcht bei den Naturvölkern* (Zutphen: W. J. Thieme und Cie, 1933), pp. v-vi.
17. United Nations, *Demographic Yearbook 1956* (New York: Statistical Office of the United Nations, 1956), Code C, pp. 47f.
18. Emile Durkheim, *Suicide: A Study in Sociology,* translated by John A. Spaulding and George Simpson (New York: Free Press of Glencoe, 1951).
19. Maurice Halbwachs, *Les causes du suicide* (Paris: Alcan, 1930).
20. Henry and Short, *op. cit.*

21. Wisse, *op. cit.*, pp. 480f.
22. Durkheim, *op. cit.*, pp. 148f.
23. John J. Honigmann, *Culture and Personality* (New York: Harper, 1954), pp. 152–54, 285–87, 310.
24. A. Irving Hallowell, "Psychic Stresses and Culture Patterns," *American Journal of Psychiatry*, XCII (May, 1936), 1291–1310.
25. Beatrice Whiting, *Paiute Sorcery*, Viking Fund Publications in Anthropology, No. 15 (New York, 1950).
26. *Ibid.*, pp. 66–81.
27. *Ibid.*, p. 74.
28. *Ibid.*, pp. 85–91.
29. Honigmann, *op. cit.*, p. 289.
30. Monica Wilson, "Witch Belief and Social Structure," *American Journal of Sociology*, LVI (1951), 307–13.
31. S. F. Nadel, "Witchcraft in Four African Societies: An Essay in Comparison," *American Anthropologist*, LIV (1952), 18–29.
32. Compare Max G. Marwick, "The Social Context of Cewa Witch Belief," *Africa*, XXII (1952), 120–35, 215–33.
33. John W. M. Whiting and Irvin L. Child, *Child Training and Personality* (New Haven: Yale University Press, 1953), pp. 263–65.
34. *Ibid.*, p. 268.
35. Clyde Kluckhohn, *Navaho Witchcraft*, Papers of the Peabody Museum, Vol. XXII, No. 2 (Cambridge, Mass.: The Museum, 1944).
36. *Ibid.*, pp. 45–72.
37. *Ibid.*, p. 55.
38. *Ibid.*, pp. 56–58.
39. *Ibid.*, pp. 60–62.
40. *Ibid.*, pp. 58–60.
41. *Ibid.*, p. 54.
42. Raoul Naroll, "A Preliminary Index of Social Development," *American Anthropologist*, LVIII (1956), 691.
43. Margaret J. Hagood and Daniel O. Price, *Statistics for Sociologists*, rev. ed. (New York: Holt, 1952), pp. 361f.
44. J. F. Kenney and E. S. Keeping, *Mathematics of Statistics*, Part Two, 2nd ed. (Princeton, N.J.: Van Nostrand, 1951), pp. 230f.
45. Donald Mainland, Lee Herrera, and Marion I. Sutcliffe, *Tables for Use with Binomial Samples* (New York: New York University College of Medicine, Department of Medical Statistics, 1956), tables 3 and 4.
46. Edmund H. Volkart and S. T. Michael, "Bereavement and Mental Health," in *Explorations in Social Psychiatry*, Alexander H. Leighton, John A. Clausen, and Robert N. Wilson, eds. (New York: Basic Books, 1957), pp. 281–307.
47. While this book was being finally made ready for the press,

there came to hand the important study, edited by Paul Bohannan, *African Homicide and Suicide* (Princeton, N.J.: Princeton University Press, 1960).

CHAPTER 4

1. William N. Fenton, *Iroquois Suicide: A Study in the Stability of a Culture Pattern,* United States Bureau of American Ethnology, Bulletin No. 128 (Washington: Government Printing Office, 1941), pp. 79–137.

2. Leland C. Wyman and Betty Thorne, "Notes on Navaho Suicide," *American Anthropologist,* XLVII (1945), 278–87.

3. Vu Cong Hoe, *Du suicide dans la société annamite* (Hanoï: Imprimerie Tonkinoise, 1937).

4. Clyde Kluckhohn, *Navaho Witchcraft,* Papers of the Peabody Museum, Vol. XXII, No. 2 (Cambridge, Mass.: The Museum, 1944).

5. Beatrice Whiting, *Paiute Sorcery,* Viking Fund Publications in Anthropology, No. 15 (New York, 1950).

6. *Ibid.*

7. John W. M. Whiting and Irvin L. Child, *Child Training and Personality,* (New Haven: Yale University Press, 1953).

8. Vu Cong Hoe, *op. cit.*

9. Williams H. R. Rivers, *The Todas* (London and New York: Macmillan, 1906).

10. See Raymond Firth, "Report on Research in Tikopia," *Oceania,* Vol. I, No. 1 (London: The Australian Research Council, 1930), 105–17; *We, the Tikopia: A Sociological Study of Kinship in Primitive Polynesia* (London: George Allen and Unwin, Ltd., 1931); "Authority and Public Opinion in Tikopia," in *Social Structure: Studies Presented to A. R. Radcliffe-Brown,* Meyer Fortes, ed. (Oxford: Clarendon Press, 1949), pp. 168–88; "Privilege Ceremonials in Tikopia," *Oceania,* Vol. XX (London: The Australian Research Council, 1951), 161–77.

11. Rivers, *op. cit.*

12. In Jakob Wisse, *Selbstmord und Todesfurcht bei den Naturvölkern* (Zutphen: W. J. Thieme und Cie, 1933), p. 20.

13. Diamond Jenness, *The Life of the Copper Eskimo,* Report of the Canadian Arctic Expedition, Vol. XII (Ottawa, 1922), pp. 1–277.

14. Knud Rasmussen, *Intellectual Culture of the Copper Eskimo,* Report of the Fifth Thule Expedition, 1921–1924, Vol. IX (Copenhagen, 1932).

15. Rivers, *op. cit.*

16. For further information see Human Relations Area Files, *Function and Scope of the Human Relations Area Files, Inc.* (New Haven: Human Relations Area Files, n.d.).

17. Harvard University Computation Laboratory, *Tables of the Cumulative Binomial Probability Distribution,* Annals of the Computation Laboratory of Harvard University, Vol. XXXV (Cambridge, Mass.: Harvard University Press, 1955).

CHAPTER 5

1. Marvin K. Opler, *Culture, Psychiatry and Human Values* (Springfield, Ill.: Charles C Thomas, 1956), p. 84.

2. Margaret Mead, *Coming of Age in Samoa,* 2nd ed. (New York: Mentor, 1949), p. 178.

3. E. C. Molina, *Poisson's Exponential Binomial Limit* (Princeton, N.J.: Van Nostrand, 1942).

4. For a full discussion, see Sinclair Smith, *Binomial, Normal and Poisson Probabilities* (Bel Air, Md.: Published by the author, 1953); compare Harvard University Computation Laboratory, *Tables of the Cumulative Binomial Probability Distribution,* Annals of the Computation Laboratory of Harvard University, Vol. XXXV (Cambridge, Mass.: Harvard University Press, 1955), p. xix.

5. Molina, *op. cit.*

6. Morice Vanoverbergh, *The Isneg Life Cycle,* Publications of the Catholic Anthropological Conference, Vol. III (Washington, 1936–1938), No. 2, pp. 81–186; No. 3, pp. 187–280.

7. Beatrice Whiting, *Paiute Sorcery,* Viking Fund Publications in Anthropology, No. 15 (New York, 1950), pp. 70f.

8. Robert Redfield, *The Folk Culture of Yucatan* (Chicago: University of Chicago Press, 1941), pp. 338f.

9. Raoul Naroll, "A Preliminary Index of Social Development," *American Anthropologist,* LVIII (1956), 687–715.

CHAPTER 6

1. Diamond Jenness, *The Life of the Copper Eskimo,* Report of the Canadian Arctic Expedition, Vol. XII (Ottawa, 1922), pp. 1–277.

2. Knud Rasmussen, *Intellectual Culture of the Copper Eskimo,* Report of the Fifth Thule Expedition, 1921–1924, Vol. IX (Copenhagen, 1932).

3. Frederck Mosteller and Robert R. Bush, "Selected Quantitative Techniques," in *Handbook of Social Psychology,* Gardner Lindzey, ed., Vol. I (Reading, Mass.: Addison-Wesley, 1954), pp. 289–334.

4. For information see Human Relations Area Files, *Function and Scope of the Human Relations Area Files, Inc.* (New Haven: Human Relations Area Files, n.d.).

5. John R. Swanton, *The Indian Tribes of North America,* Bureau

of American Ethnology, Bulletin No. 145 (Washington: Government Printing Office, 1952).

6. Julian H. Steward, ed., *Handbook of South American Indians*, 6 Vols., Bureau of American Ethnology, Bulletin No. 143 (Washington: Government Printing Office, 1946-50).

7. Frederick E. Croxton and Dudley J. Cowden, *Applied General Statistics* (Englewood Cliffs, N.J.: Prentice-Hall, 1939), pp. 344-48, extrapolating horizontally on Table G1.

8. Margaret J. Hagood and Daniel O. Price, *Statistics for Sociologists*, rev. ed. (New York: Holt, 1952), pp. 248f.

9. J. F. Kenney and E. S. Keeping, *Mathematics of Statistics, Part Two*, 2nd ed. (Princeton, N.J.: Van Nostrand, 1951), Theorem 1.13.

CHAPTER 7

1. Martin Reif, MS.

2. William H. R. Rivers, *The Todas* (London and New York: Macmillan, 1906), pp. 476, 455.

3. Curt Nimuendaju, *The Eastern Timbira*, translated by Robert H. Lowie, University of California Publications in American Archeology and Ethnology, Vol. XLI (Berkeley: University of California Press, 1946), p. 129, 160.

4. E. Maurel, "Mission to Cambodia," *Popular Science Monthly*, XXX (New York, 1887), 316.

5. Virginia Thompson, *French Indo-China* (New York: Macmillan, 1937), p. 348.

6. Hans H. Brüning, "Reisen im Gebiet der Aguaruna," *Baessler Archiv*, XII (Berlin: Reimer, 1928), 55.

7. Kunio Odaka, *Economic Organization of the Li Tribes of Hainan Island*, Yale University Southeast Studies of Asia Translation Series (New Haven: Yale University Press, 1950), pp. 27f, 60.

8. Pierre Gourou, *Les paysans du delta tonkinois. Étude de géographie humaine*. Publications de l'Ecole Française-d'Extreme-Orient, Vol. XXV, Edition d'Art et d'Histoire (Paris, 1936), pp. 460, 525-28.

9. P. C. Richard, "Notes pour servir à l'Ethnographie de la Cochinchine," *Revue maritime et coloniale*, XXI (Paris: Challamel Aîné, 1867), 111.

10. R. S. Rattray, *Ashanti* (Oxford: Clarendon, 1923), p. 135; and *Ashanti Law and Constitution* (Oxford: Clarendon, 1929), p. 329.

11. Beatrice Whiting, *Paiute Sorcery*, Viking Fund Publications in Anthropology, No. 15 (New York, 1950), p. 61.

12. Verne F. Ray, *The Sanpoil and Nespelem: Salishan People of Northeastern Washington* (Seattle: University of Washington Press, 1933), p. 329.

13. United Nations, *Demographic Yearbook 1956* (New York: Statistical Office of the United Nations, 1956).

14. Ivan E. P. Veniaminov, *Notes on the Islands of the Unalaska District*, Vol. III (St. Petersburg: Russian American Company, 1840a), p. 55.

15. Ralph Linton, *The Tanala: A Hill Tribe of Madagascar*, Publications of Field Museum of Natural History Anthropological Series, Vol. XXII (Chicago, 1933), p. 155.

16. William H. Hudspeth, *Stone Gateway and the Flowery Miao* (London: The Cargate Press, 1937), pp. 43f.

17. United Nations, *op. cit.*

18. B. Whiting, *op. cit.*, pp. 62f, 76–78.

19. Ray, *loc. cit.*

20. Richard Van Valkenburgh, *Navaho Common Law: Notes on Political Organization, Property and Inheritance*, Museum Notes, Museum of Northern Arizona, IX (Flagstaff: Northern Arizona Society of Science and Art, Inc., 1936), p. 52.

21. Hudspeth, *loc. cit.*

22. Allan R. Holmberg, *Nomads of the Long Bow: The Siriono of Eastern Bolivia*, Smithsonian Institute: Institute of Social Anthropology, Publication No. 10 (Washington: Government Printing Office, 1950), pp. 60f.

23. David B. Stout, *San Blas Cuna Acculturation: An Introduction*, Viking Fund Publications in Anthropology, No. 14 (New York, 1947), pp. 30f.

24. James Owen Dorsey, *Omaha Dwellings, Furniture and Implements*, Thirteenth Annual Report of the Bureau of Ethnology, 1891–1892 (Washington: Government Printing Office, 1896), p. 370.

25. Ruth Landes, "The Ojibwa of Canada," in *Cooperation and Competition among Primitive Peoples*, Margaret Mead, ed. (New York and London: McGraw-Hill, 1937), p. 109.

26. W. Vernon Kinietz, *Chippewa Village: The Story of Katikitegon*, Cranbrook Institute of Science, Bulletin No. 25 (Bloomfield Hills, Mich.: Cranbrook Press, 1947), pp. 140–2.

27. Lewis Henry Morgan, *League of the HO-DE-NO-SAU-NEE or Iroquois*, 2 Vols., Herbert M. Lloyd, ed. and annotator (New York: Dodd, Mead, 1901), pp. 133, 321.

28. William N. Fenton, *Iroquois Suicide: A Study in the Stability of a Culture Pattern*, United States Bureau of American Ethnology, Bulletin No. 128 (Washington: Government Printing Office, 1941), pp. 90, 120f.

29. Thompson, *op. cit.*, p. 365.

30. Mauricio de Heriarte, *Descripcao de Estado do Maranhae, Para, Corupa et Rio das Amazonas* (Vienna: Imperial Library, 1847), p. 16.

31. Fernao Cardim, "A Treatise of Brazil . . . ," in Samuel Purchas, ed., and trans., *Hakluytus Posthumus or Purchas His Pilgrimes* (Glasgow: James MacLehose, 1906, 20 vols.), Vol. XVI, pp. 417–517.

32. Knud Rasmussen, *Intellectual Culture of the Copper Eskimo,* Report of the Fifth Thule Expedition, 1921–1924, Vol. IX (Copenhagen, 1932).

33. Diamond Jenness, *The Life of the Copper Eskimo,* Report of the Canadian Arctic Expedition, Vol. XII (Ottawa, 1922), pp. 1–277.

34. B. Whiting, *op. cit.,* pp. 70f.

35. Linton, *op. cit.,* p. 313.

36. P. M. Larken, "An Account of the Zande," *Sudan Notes and Records,* IX (Khartoum: McCorquodale and Co., 1926–1927), 17.

37. United Nations, *op. cit.*

38. Jakob Wisse, *Selbstmord und Todesfurcht bei den Naturvölkern* (Zutphen: W. J. Thieme und Cie, 1933), pp. 466–70.

39. United Nations, *op. cit.*

40. Martin Gusinde, *Die Feuerland Indianer,* Vol. I (Mödling bei Wien: Anthropos, 1931 *et seq.*), pp. 144–49.

41. John M. Cooper, *An Analytical and Critical Bibliography of the Tribes of Tierra del Fuego and Adjacent Territory,* Bureau of American Ethnology, Bulletin No. 63 (Washington: Government Printing Office, 1917).

42. Gusinde, *op. cit.,* pp. 481, 1119.

43. Cooper, *op. cit.,* p. 175.

44. Alés Hrdlícka, *Physiological and Medical Observations among the Indians of Southwest United States and Northern Mexico,* Smithsonian Institute, Bureau of American Ethnology, Bulletin No. 34 (Washington: Government Printing Office, 1908), pp. 5–7, 171.

45. George Scott Robertson, *The Kafirs of the Hindu-Kush* (London: Lawrence and Bullen, 1900), p. 381.

46. Elizabeth Bacon, "Kafirs," in *Encyclopedia Americana,* Vol. XVI (1958), p. 276.

47. P. von Stenin, "Die Kirgisen des Kreises Saissansk im Gebiete von Ssemi-palatinsk," *Globus,* LXIX (1896), pp. 227–30.

48. Von Stenin, *op. cit.,* p. 230.

49. Erminie W. Voegelin, "Suicide in Northeastern California," *American Anthropologist,* XXXIX (1937), pp. 445–56.

50. *Ibid.,* pp. 454f.

51. *Ibid.,* pp. 453f.

52. *Ibid.,* p. 454.

53. *Ibid.,* p. 452.

54. *Ibid.,* p. 453.

55. B. Whiting, *op. cit.,* pp. 70f.

56. Rivers, *op. cit.,* p. 555.

57. Vu Cong Hoe, *Du suicide dans la société annamite* (Hanoï: Imprimerie Tonkinoise, 1937), pp. 4, 6.

58. Fenton, *op. cit.*

59. Leland C. Wyman and Betty Thorne, "Notes on Navaho Suicide," *American Anthropologist*, XLVII (1945), 278f.

60. Morice Vanoverbergh, *The Isneg Life Cycle*, Publications of the Catholic Anthropological Conference, Vol. III, No. 3 (Washington, 1936-8), p. 238.

61. Linton, *op. cit.*, p. 313.

62. Larken, *op. cit.*, p. 17.

63. David Crockett Graham, "The Customs of the Ch'uan Miao," *Journal of the West China Border Research Society*, IX (1937), 40.

64. Hudspeth, *op. cit.*, pp. 43f.

65. See Wilfred D. Hambly, *The Ovimbundu of Angola*, Field Museum of Natural History, Anthropological Series, Vol. XXI, No. 2 (Chicago, 1934), p. 125.

66. Harry A. Franck, *East of Siam, Ramblings in the Five Divisions of French Indo-China* (New York: Century, 1926), pp. 81f.

67. Thompson, *op. cit.*, p. 325.

68. J. Robert Moose, *Village Life in Korea* (Nashville: M. E. Church, 1911), pp. 110f.

69. William E. Griffis, *Corea, The Hermit Nation* (New York: Charles Scribner's Sons, 1882), p. 255.

70. Earnest Beaglehole and Pearl Beaglehole, *Ethnology of Pukapuka*, Bernice P. Bishop Museum Bulletin No. 150 (Honolulu, 1938), p. 373; *Myths, Stories and Chants from Pukapuka*, MS. on file at Bernice P. Bishop Museum (Honolulu, n.d.), pp. 53f.

71. Gabriel Soares de Souza, "Tratado descriptive do Brazil em 1587," *Revista do Instituto Historico e Geographico do Brazil*, IX (1851), pp. 323.

72. Ray, *op. cit.*, p. 149.

73. Günter Tessman, *Die Indianer Nordost-Perus* (Hamburg: Friederichsen, 1930), p. 362.

74. Rafael Karsten, *The Head Hunters of Western Amazonas: The Life and Culture of the Jibaro Indians of Eastern Ecuador and Peru*, Commentationes Humanarum Litterarum, Vol. VII, No. 1 (Helsingfors: Centraltryckeriet Societas Scientarum Fennica, 1935), p. 223.

75. Paul Rivet, "Les Indiens Jibaros: Etude géographique, historique et ethnographique," *L'Anthropologie*, XVIII (Paris: Masson et Cie., 1907), p. 239.

76. Brüning, *op. cit.*, p. 50.

77. Alois Musil, *The Manners and Customs of the Rwala Bedouins*, The American Geographical Society, Oriental Explorations and Studies, No. 6 (New York, 1928), p. 240.

78. Jenness, *op. cit.*, p. 233.
79. Rasmussen, *op. cit.*, pp. 46f.
80. Jenness, *op. cit.*
81. Rasmussen, *op. cit.*
82. Veniaminov, *op. cit.*, pp. 28f, 32f.
83. Ivan E. P. Veniaminov, *Notes on the Athin Aleuts and the Koloshi* (St. Petersburg: Russian American Company, 1840b), pp. 8f.
84. Wisse, *op. cit.*, p. 426.
85. Raymond Firth, "Report on Research in Tikopia," *Oceania*, Vol. I, No. 1 (London: The Australian Research Council, 1930), 90; *We, the Tikopia: A Sociological Study of Kinship in Primitive Polynesia* (London: George Allen and Unwin, Ltd., 1931), pp. 514f; "Authority and Public Opinion in Tikopia," *Social Structure: Studies Presented to A. R. Radcliffe-Brown*, Meyer Fortes, ed. (Oxford: Clarendon Press, 1949), p. 180; "Privilege Ceremonials in Tikopia," *Oceania*, XX (London: The Australian Research Council, 1951), 168.
86. Clyde Kluckhohn, *Navaho Witchcraft*, Papers of the Peabody Museum, Vol. XXII, No. 2 (Cambridge, Mass.: The Museum, 1944).
87. B. Whiting, *op. cit.*, pp. 85, 87.
88. John W. M. Whiting and Irvin L. Child, *Child Training and Personality* (New Haven: Yale University Press, 1953), pp. 344ff.
89. B. Whiting, *op. cit.*
90. Whiting and Child, *op. cit.*

Bibliography

American Anthropological Association, Executive Board. "Statement on Human Rights," *American Anthropologist,* XLIX (1947), 539–43.

American Standards Association. *Control Chart Method of Controlling Quality during Production.* Pamphlet Z1.3. New York: American Standards Association, 1942.

Arsenian, John, and Jean M. Arsenian. "Tough and Easy Cultures," *Psychiatry,* II (1948), 337–85.

Bacon, Elizabeth. "Kafirs," in *Encyclopedia Americana,* Vol. XVI (1958), 276.

Bales, Robert. "Cultural Differences in Rates of Alcoholism," *Quarterly Journal of Studies on Alcohol,* VI (1946), 480–99.

Barton, Roy F. *Ifugao Law.* Berkeley: University of California Press, 1919.

———. *Ifugao Economics.* Berkeley: University of California Press, 1922.

Beaglehole, Earnest, and Pearl Beaglehole. *Ethnology of Pukapuka.* Bernice P. Bishop Museum Bulletin No. 150. Honolulu: Bernice P. Bishop Museum, 1938.

——— and ———. *Myths, Stories and Chants from Pukapuka.* MS. on file at Bernice P. Bishop Museum, Honolulu, n.d.

Beard, Charles A. "That Noble Dream," *American Historical Review*, XLI (1935), 74–87.

————. "Written History as an Act of Faith," *American Historical Review*, XXXIX (1934) 219–29.

Benedict, Ruth. *Patterns of Culture*. New York: Mentor Books, 1946.

Berelson, Bernard. "Content Analysis," in *Handbook of Social Psychology*, Gardner Lindzey, ed. Reading, Mass.: Addison-Wesley, 1954, I:488–522.

Bergman, Sten. *In Korean Wilds and Villages*. London: John Gifford, 1938.

Bernheim, Ernst. *Lehrbuch der historischen Methode und der Geschichtsphilosophie*. 6th ed. Munich and Leipzig: Duncker and Humblot, 1908.

Boas, Franz. "Anthropology and Statistics," in *The Social Sciences and Their Interrelations*. W. F. Ogburn and A. Goldenweiser, eds. Boston: Houghton Mifflin, 1927, pp. 114–21.

Bohannan, Paul, ed. *African Homicide and Suicide*. Princeton, N.J.: Princeton University Press, 1960.

Brearly, H. C. *Homicide in the United States*. Chapel Hill, N.C.: University of North Carolina Press, 1932.

Brüning, Hans H. "Reisen im Gebiet der Aguaruna," *Baessler Archiv*, XII (1928), 46–85. Berlin: Reimer.

Buel, Clarence C., and Robert V. Johnson, eds. *Battles and Leaders of the Civil War*. New York: 1887, 4 vols.

Bullen, Adelaide. "A Cross-Cultural Approach to the Problem of Stuttering," *Child Development*, XVI (1945, 1–88.

Burrows, Edwin Grant. *The People of Ifalik: A Little-Disturbed Atoll Culture*. Unpublished MS. submitted as a final report, Coordinated Investigation of Micronesian Anthropology. Washington: Science Board, National Research Council, 1949.

Cardim, Fernao. "A Treatise of Brazil . . . ," in *Hakluytus Posthumus or Purchas his Pilgrimes*, Samuel Purchas, ed. and trans. Glasgow: James MacLehose, 1906, Vol. XVI, pp. 417–517.

Casati, Gaetano. *Ten Years in Equatoria and the Return with Emin Pasha*, Vol. II. Mrs. J. Randolph Clay assisted by I. Walter

Savage, translator. London and New York: Frederick Warne, 1891.

Childs, Gladwyn Murray. *Umbundu Kinship and Character.* London and New York: International African Institute and the Witwatersrand University Press, 1949.

Coleman, James C. *Abnormal Psychology and Modern Life.* New York: Scott, Foresman, 1950.

Coon, Carleton S. *A Reader in General Anthropology.* New York: Holt, 1948.

Cooper, John M. *An Analytical and Critical Bibliography of the Tribes of Tierra del Fuego and Adjacent Territory.* Bureau of American Ethnology, Bulletin No. 63. Washington: Government Printing Office, 1917.

Coxe, William. *Account of the Russian Discoveries between Asia and America, to which are added the conquest of Siberia and the History of the Transactions and Commerce with China.* London: Cadell and Davies, 1804.

Croce, Benedetto. *History: Its Theory and Practice.* Douglas Ainslee, translator. New York: Harcourt Brace, 1921.

Croxton, Frederick E., and Dudley J. Cowden. *Applied General Statistics.* Englewood Cliffs, N.J.: Prentice-Hall, 1939.

Czekanowski, Jan. *Forschungen im Nil-Kongo Zwischengebiet.* Wissenschaftliche Ergebenisse der Deutschen Zentral Afrika-Expedition, 1907–1908, Vol. II. Leipzig: Klinkhardt und Bierman, 1924.

Daguio, Amador T. *Hudhud Hi Aliguyon: A Translation of an Ifugao Harvest Song with Introduction and Notes.* Unpublished Master's Thesis, Stanford University Library, 1952.

Davie, Maurice R. *The Evolution of War*, Vol. I. New Haven: Yale University Press, 1929.

DePuyt, Lucien. "Account of Scientific Exploration in the Isthmus of Darien in the Years 1861 and 1865," *The Journal of Royal Geography*, XXXVIII 1868), 69–110. London: John Murray.

d'Evreux, Yves. *Voyage dans le Nord du Brésil fait durant les années 1613 et 1614.* Paris and Leipzig: A. Franck, 1864.

Dorsey, James Owen. *Omaha Dwellings, Furniture and Implements.* Thirteenth Annual Report of the Bureau of Ethnology, 1891–1892. Washington: Government Printing Office, 1896, pp. 263–88.

Driver, Harold E. "An Integration of Functional, Evolutionary and Historical Theory by Means of Correlations," *International Journal of American Linguistics,* Memoir 12 (1956), 1–36. Indiana Publications in Anthropology and Linguistics.

Duncan, Acheson J. *Quality Control and Industrial Statistics.* Homewood, Ill.: Irwin, 1955.

Durkheim, Émile. *Suicide: A Study in Sociology.* John A. Spaulding and George Simpson, translators. New York: Free Press of Glencoe, 1951.

East, Rupert, ed. *Akiga's Own Story: The Tiv Tribe, as Seen by One of Its Members.* London: The International Institute of African Languages and Cultures, Oxford University Press, 1939.

Eaton, Joseph W., and Robert J. Weil. *Culture and Mental Disorders: A Comparative Study of Hutterites and Other Population.* New York: Free Press of Glencoe, 1955.

Elliot, Henry Wood. *Our Arctic Province.* New York: Scribner's Sons, 1886.

Evans-Pritchard, Edward Evan. *Witchcraft, Oracles and Magic among the Azande.* Oxford: Clarendon Press, 1937.

Fenton, William N. *Iroquois Suicide: A Study in the Stability of a Culture Pattern.* United States Bureau of American Ethnology, Bulletin No. 128. Washington: Government Printing Office, 1941, pp. 79–137.

Firth, Raymond. "Report on Research in Tikopia," *Oceania,* Vol. I, No. 1 (1930), 105–17. London: The Australian Research Council.

———. *We, The Tikopia: A Sociological Study of Kinship in Primitive Polynesia.* London: George Allen and Unwin, Ltd., 1931.

———. *Primitive Polynesian Economy.* London: George Routledge and Sons, Ltd., 1939.

———. "Authority and Public Opinion in Tikopia," in *Social Structure: Studies Presented to A. R. Radcliffe-Brown,* Meyer Fortes, ed. Oxford: Clarendon Press, 1949, pp. 168–88.

———. "Privilege Ceremonials in Tikopia," *Oceania,* XX (1951), 161–77. London: The Australian Research Council.

Fletcher, Alice C., and Francis LaFleche. *The Omaha Tribe.* Twenty-seventh Annual Report of the Bureau of American Ethnology, 1905–1906. Washington: Government Printing Office, 1911.

Ford, Clellan S. *A Comparative Study of Human Reproduction.* Yale University Publications in Anthropolgy No. 32. New Haven: Yale University Press, 1945.

———, and Frank A. Beach. *Patterns of Sexual Behavior.* New York: Harper, 1953.

Forde, C. Daryll. *Habitat, Economy and Society.* London: Methuen, 1937.

Fortune, Reo F. *Omaha Secret Societies.* New York: Columbia University Press, 1932.

Franck, Harry A. *East of Siam: Ramblings in the Five Divisions of French Indo-China.* New York: The Century Co., 1926.

Frazer, James G. *The Golden Bough.* 3rd ed., 12 Vols. London: Macmillan, 1911–1915.

Gillin, John. *The Barama River Caribs of British Guiana.* Papers of the Peabody Society of American Archeology and Ethnology, Vol. XIV, No. 2. Cambridge, Mass., 1936.

Goodenough, Florence L. *Exceptional Children.* New York: Appleton-Century-Crofts, 1956.

Goodenough, Ward H. "Residence Rules," *Southwestern Journal of Anthropology,* XII (1956), 22–37.

Gourou, Pierre. *Les paysans du delta tonkinois: Étude de géographie humaine.* Publications de l'Éole Française d'Extrême-Orient, Vol. XXV, Edition d'Art et d'Histoire. Paris, 1936.

———. *Land Utilization in French Indo-China.* Washington: Institute of Pacific Relations, 1945.

Graham, David Crockett. "The Customs of the Ch'uan Miao," *Journal of the West China Border Research Society,* IX (1937), 13–70. Shanghai: Thomas Chou and Sons.

Griffis, William E. *Corea, The Hermit Nation.* New York: Scribner's Sons, 1882.

Gurdon, P. R. T. *The Khasis.* London: David Nutt, 1907.

Gusinde, Martin. *Die Feuerland Indianer,* Vol. I. Mödling bei Wien, Anthropos, 1931 *et seq.*

Gutmann, Bruno. *Das Recht der Dschagga.* Arbeiten zur Entwicklungspsychologie No. 7. Munich: C. H. Beck, 1926, pp. 1–733.

Hagood, Margaret J., and Daniel O. Price. *Statistics for Sociologists.* Rev. ed. New York: Holt, 1952.

Halbwachs, Maurice. *Les causes du suicide.* Paris: Alcan, 1930.

Hallowell, A. Irving. "Psychic Stresses and Culture Patterns," *American Journal of Psychiatry,* XCII (May, 1936), 1291–1310.

Hambly, Wilfred D. *The Ovimbundu of Angola.* Field Museum of Natural History, Anthropological Series, Vol. XXI, No. 2. Chicago, 1934, pp. 87–362.

Harvard University Computation Laboratory. *Tables of the Cumulative Binomial Probability Distribution.* Annals of the Computation Laboratory of Harvard University, Vol. XXXV. Cambridge, Mass.: Harvard University Press, 1955.

Henry, Andrew F., and James F. Short, Jr., *Suicide and Homicide.* New York: Free Press of Glencoe, 1954.

Heriarte, Mauricio de. *Descripao do Estado do Maranhao, Para, Corupa et Rio das Amazonas.* Vienna: Imperial Library, 1847.

Herskovits, Melville J. *Economic Anthropology: A Study in Comparative Economics.* New York: Knopf, 1952.

Hockett, Homer C. *The Critical Method in Historical Research and Writing.* New York: Macmillan, 1955.

Holmberg, Allan R. *Nomads of the Long Bow: The Siriono of Eastern Bolivia.* Smithsonian Institute: Institute of Social Anthropology Publication No. 10. Washington: Government Printing Office, 1950.

Homans, George C., and David M. Schneider. *Marriage, Authority and Final Causes.* New York: Free Press of Glencoe, 1955.

Honigmann, John J. *Culture and Personality.* New York: Harper, 1954.

Horton, Donald. "The Functions of Alcohol in Primitive

Societies: A Cross-Cultural survey," *Quarterly Journal of Studies on Alcohol,* IV (1943), 199–320.

Hrdlićka, Alés. *Physiological and Medical Observations among the Indians of Southwest United States and Northern Mexico.* Smithsonian Institute, Bureau of American Ethnology, Bulletin 34. Washington: Government Printing Office, 1908.

————. *The Aleutian and Commander Islands and Their Inhabitants.* Philadelphia: Wistar Institute of Anatomy and Biology, 1945.

Hudspeth, William H. *Stone Gateway and the Flowery Miao.* London: The Cargate Press, 1937.

Jackson, Don. D. "Theories of Suicide," in *Clues to Suicide,* Edwin S. Schneidman and N. L. Farberow, eds. New York: McGraw-Hill, 1957, pp. 11–21.

Jenness, Diamond. *The Life of the Copper Eskimo.* Report of the Canadian Arctic Expedition, Vol. XII. Ottawa, 1922, pp. 1–277.

Junod, Henri A. *The Life of a South African Tribe,* Vol. I. London: Macmillan and Co., 1927.

Karsten, Rafael. *The Head Hunters of Western Amazonas: The Life and Culture of the Jibaro Indians of Eastern Ecuador and Peru.* Commentationes Humanarum Litterarum, Vol. VII, No. 1. Helsingfors: Centraltryckeriet Societas Scientarum Fennica, 1935.

Kenney, J. F., and E. S. Keeping. *Mathematics of Statistics,* Part Two. 2nd ed. Princeton, N.J.: Van Nostrand, 1951.

Kinietz, W. Vernon. *Chippewa Village: The Story of Katikitegon.* Cranbrook Institute of Science, Bulletin No. 25. Bloomfield Hills, Mich.: Cranbrook Press, 1947.

Kluckhohn, Clyde. *Navaho Witchcraft.* Papers of the Peabody Museum, Vol. XXII, No. 2. Cambridge, Mass.: The Museum, 1944.

————. "Group Tensions: Analysis of a Case History," in *Approaches to National Unity.* New York: The Conference on Science, Religion and Philosophy in Their Relation to the Democratic Way of Life, Fifth Symposium, 1945, pp. 222–43.

Köbben, Andre J. "New Ways of Presenting an Old Idea: The

Statistical Method in Social Anthropology," *Journal of the Royal Anthropological Institute,* LXXXII (1952), 129–46. Reprinted in Moore, pp. 175–192.

Landes, Ruth. "The Ojibwa of Canada," in *Cooperation and Competition among Primitive Peoples,* Margaret Mead, ed. New York and London: McGraw-Hill, 1937, pp. 87–126.

Langlois, Charles V. and C. Seignobos. *Introduction to the Study of History.* Translated by G. G. Berry. New York: Henry Holt and Co., 1898.

Larken, P. M. "An Account of the Zande," *Sudan Notes and Records,* IX (1926), 1–55, X (1927), 85–134. Khartoum: McCorquodale and Co.

Lazarsfeld, Paul F., and Morris Rosenberg. *The Language of Social Research.* New York: Free Press of Glencoe, 1955.

Lemert, Edwin M. *Social Pathology.* New York: McGraw-Hill, 1951.

————. "Some Indians Who Stutter," *Journal of Speech and Hearing Disorders,* XVIII (1953), 168–74.

————. "Alcoholism and the Sociocultural Situation," *Quarterly Journal of Studies on Alcohol,* XVII (1956), 306–17.

Levi, Carlo. *Christ Stopped at Eboli.* Translated by Frances Frenaye. New York: Farrar, Strauss, 1950.

Linton, Ralph. *The Tanala: A Hill Tribe of Madagascar.* Publications of Field Museum of Natural History Anthropological Series, Vol. XXII. Chicago, 1933.

Lowie, Robert H. "Evolution in Cultural Anthropology: A Reply to Leslie White," *American Anthropologist,* XLVIII (1946), 223–33.

Madow, William G. "Review of 'Introduction to Statistical Reasoning,'" *Journal of the American Statistical Association,* LIII (1958), 208–12.

Magalhaes de Gandavo. *Treatise on the Land of Brazil. Documents and Narratives Concerning the Discovery and Conquest of Latin America.* The Histories of Brazil, Vol. XI. New York: The Cortes Society, pp. 125–232.

Mainland, Donald, Lee Herrera, and Marion I. Sutcliffe.

Tables for Use with Binomial Samples. New York: New York University College of Medicine, Department of Medical Statistics, 1956.

Marshall, Donald Stanley. *Cuna Folk: A Conceptual Scheme as Applied to the Cuna Indians of Darien.* Unpublished MS. presented to Department of Anthropology, Harvard University, 1950.

Marwick, Max G. "The Social Context of Cewa Witchcraft," *Africa,* XXII (1952), 120–35, 215–33.

Maurel, E. "Mission to Cambodia," *Popular Science Monthly,* XXX (1887), 310–22. New York.

Mead, Margaret. *Coming of Age in Samoa,* 2nd ed. New York: Mentor, 1949.

———, ed. *Cooperation and Competition among Primitive Peoples.* New York: McGraw-Hill, 1937.

Mensel, Herbert. "Comment on Robinson's 'Ecological Correlations and the Behavior of Individuals,'" *American Sociological Review,* XV (1950), 674.

Moore, Frank W., ed. *Readings in Cross-Cultural Methodology* (New Haven: HRAF Press, 1961). N.B. This collection of readings includes reprints of important papers, cited in this bibliography, by Tylor, Murdock, Köbben, Lewis, Whiting, Moore, and Naroll.

Molina, E. C. *Poisson's Exponential Binomial Limit.* Princeton, N.J.: Van Nostrand, 1942.

Moose, J. Robert. *Village Life in Korea.* Nashville: M. E. Church, 1911.

Morgan, Lewis Henry. *League of the HO-DE-NO-SAU-NEE or Iroquois,* 2 Vols. Herbert M. Lloyd, ed. and annotator. New York: Dodd, Mead, 1901.

Moses, Lincoln E. "Nonparametric Statistics for Psychological Research," *Psychological Bulletin,* XLIX (1952), 122–43.

Mosteller, Frederick, and Robert R. Bush. "Selected Quantitative Techniques," in *Handbook of Social Psychology,* Vol. I, Gardner Lindzey, ed. Reading, Mass.: Addison-Wesley, 1954, pp. 289–334.

Murdock, George P. "The Common Denominator of Cultures," in *Science of Man in the World Crisis,* Ralph Linton, ed. New York: Columbia University Press, 1945, pp. 123–42.

————. *Social Structure.* New York: Macmillan, 1949.

————. *Outline of World Cultures.* New Haven: Human Relations Area Files, 1954.

————. "World Ethnographic Sample," *American Anthropologist,* LIX (1957), 664–87. Reprinted in Moore, *supra,* pp. 193–216.

————, and John W. M. Whiting. "Cultural Determination of Parental Attitudes," in *Problems of Infancy and Childhood, Transactions of the Fourth Conference . . . 1950,* Milton J. E. Senn, ed. New York: Macy Foundation, 1951, pp. 13–80.

Musil, Alois. *The Manners and Customs of the Rwala Bedouins.* The American Geographical Society, Oriental Explorations and Studies, No. 6. New York, 1928.

Nadel, S. F. "Witchcraft in Four African Societies: An Essay in Comparison," *American Anthropologist,* LIV (1952), 18–29.

Naroll, Frada, Raoul Naroll, and Forrest Howard, "Position of Women in Childbirth: A Study in Data Quality Control," *American Journal of Obstetrics and Gynecology,* Vol. 82 (1961), 943–54.

Naroll, Raoul. "Sheridan and Cedar Creek: A Reappraisal," *Military Affairs,* XVI (1952), 153–68.

————. "Lincoln and the Sherman Peace Fiasco—Another Fable?" *Journal of Southern History,* XX (1954), 459–83.

————. "A Preliminary Index of Social Development," *American Anthropologist,* LVIII (1956), 687–715.

————. "A Tentative Index of Culture Stress," *International Journal of Social Psychiatry,* V (1959) 107–16.

————. "Controlling Data Quality," Series Research in Social Psychology, *Symposia Studies Series,* Volume 4, National Institute of Social and Behavioral Sciences, September, 1960.

————. "Two Solutions to Galton's Problem," *Philosophy of Science,* Vol. 28, No. 1 (1961), pp. 15–39. Reprinted in Moore, *supra,* pp. 217–42.

————. "Historians and Laws of History," *American Anthropogist,* LV (1953) 450f.

————. "German Kinship Terms," *American Anthropologist,* LX (1958) 750–55.

Nimuendaju, Curt. *The Eastern Timbira.* Translated by Robert H. Lowie. University of California Publications in American Archeology and Ethnology, Vol. XLI. Berkeley: University of California Press, 1946.

Odaka, Kunio. *Economic Organization of the Li Tribes of Hainan Island.* Yale University Southeast Studies of Asia Translation Series. New Haven: Yale University Press, 1950.

Opler, Marvin K. *Culture, Psychiatry and Human Values.* Springfield, Ill.: Charles C Thomas, 1956.

Parker, Arthur C. *The Code of Handsome Lake, the Seneca Prophet.* New York State Museum Bulletin 163. Albany: University of the State of New York, 1913.

Pierce, Albert. "The Classification of Documents Relative to Source Proximity," paper read at the public Anthropological Conference sponsored by the Southwestern Anthropological Association and the Wenner-Gren Foundation for Anthropological Research at the University of California, Los Angeles, April 25, 1959.

Popper, Karl. *Logik der Forschung: sur Erkenntnisstheorie der Modernen Naturwissenschaft.* Vienna: Julius Springer, 1935.

Porée, Guy, and Eveline Maspero. *Moeurs et coutumes des Khmers.* Paris: Payot, 1938.

Rasmussen, Knud. *Intellectual Culture of the Copper Eskimo.* Report of the Fifth Thule Expedition, 1921–1924, Vol. IX. Copenhagen, 1932.

Rattray, R. S. *Ashanti.* Oxford: Clarendon Press, 1923.

————. *Ashanti Law and Constitution.* Oxford: Clarendon Press, 1929.

Raum, O. F. *A Description of Indigenous Education in an East African Tribe.* London: Oxford University Press for the International Institute for African Languages and Customs, 1940.

Ray, Verne F. *The Sanpoil and Nespelem: Salishan People of Northeastern Washington.* Seattle: University of Washington Press, 1933.

Redfield, Robert. *The Folk Culture of Yucatan.* Chicago: University of Chicago Press, 1941.

Richard, P. C. "Notes pour servir à l'ethnographie de la Cochinchine," *Revue maritime et coloniale,* XXI (1867), 92–133. Paris: Challamel Aîné.

Rivers, William H. R. *The Todas.* London and New York: Macmillan, 1906.

––––––. *The History of Melanesian Society,* Vol. I. Cambridge: Cambridge University Press, 1914.

Rivet, Paul. "Les Indiens Jibaros: Étude géographique, historique et ethnographique," *L'Anthropologie,* XVIII (1907), 333–68, 583–618. Paris: Masson et Cie.

Robequain, Charles. *The Economic Development of French Indo-China.* London: Oxford University Press, 1944.

Robertson, George Scott, *The Kafirs of the Hindu-Kush.* London: Lawrence and Bullen, 1900.

Robinson, William S. "Ecological Correlations and the Behavior of Individuals," *American Sociological Review,* XV (1950), 351–57.

St. Louis, City of. *Sixty-Second Annual Report of the Board of Education of the City of St. Louis, Missouri, for the year ending June 30, 1916.* St. Louis, Mo., 1916.

Sarytschew (Sarychev), Gawrila. *Account of a Voyage of Discovery to the Northeast of Siberia,* Vol. II. London: Richard Phillips, 1806.

Savage, I. Richard. "Bibliography of Nonparametric Statistics and Related Topics," *Journal of the American Statistical Association,* LXVIII (1953), 844–906.

Schapera, I. "Some Comments on Comparative Method in Social Anthropology," *American Anthropologist,* LV (1953), 353–61.

Schmidt, Wilhelm. *The Culture Historical Method of Ethnology.* Translated by S. A. Sieber. New York: Fortuny's, 1937–1939.

Schneider, Ernst. *Über das Stottern.* Beiheft zur Schweizerischen Zeitschrift für Psychologie und ihre Anwendungen No. 22. Bern and Stuttgart: Huber, 1953.

Schneider, Pierre B. *La tentative de suicide: Étude statistique, clinique, psychologique et catamnestique.* Paris and Neuchatel: Delachaux, 1954.

Selye, Hans. *The Stress of Life.* New York: McGraw-Hill, 1956.

Simmons, Leo W., and Harold G. Wolff. *Social Science in Medicine.* New York: Russell Sage Foundation, 1954.

Smith, Ed Sinclair. *Binomial, Normal and Poisson Probabilities.* Bel Air, Md.: Published by the author, 1953.

Snidecor, John C. "Why the Indian Does Not Stutter," *Quarterly Journal of Speech,* XXXIII (1947), 493–95.

Snyder, Charles R. "Culture and Sobriety: A Study of Drinking Factors Related to Sobriety among Jews," *Quarterly Journal of Studies on Alcohol,* XVI (1955), 101–77.

Soares de Souza, Gabriel. "Tratado descriptivo do Brazil em 1587," *Revista do Instituto Historico e Geographico do Brazil,* XIV (1851), 1–423.

Spiro, Melford E. *Ifaluk: A South Sea Culture.* Unpublished MS submitted as a final report, Coordinated Investigation of Micronesian Anthropology. Washington: Pacific Science Board, National Research Council, 1949.

———. "A Psychotic Personality in the South Seas," *Psychiatry,* Vol. XIII, No. 2. Washington: William Alanson White Psychiatric Foundation, 1950, pp. 189–204.

Statistical Research Group, Columbia University. *Sequential Analysis of Statistical Data: Applications,* rev. ed. New York: Columbia University Press, 1946.

Stefansson, Vilhjalmur. *My Life with the Eskimo.* New York: Macmillan, 1913.

Stegmiller, P. F. "Aus dem religiosen Leben der Khasi," *Anthropos,* XVI (1921), 407-41.

———. "Opfer und Opferbraeuche der Khase," *Mitteilungen der Anthropologischen Gesellschaft in Wien,* LIV (1924), 211–31.

Steinmetz, Rudolf S. "Endokannibalismus," *Mittheilungen der Anthropologischen Gesellschaft in Wien,* XXVI (1896), 1–60. Reprinted in *Gesammelte Kleinere Schriften zur Ethnologie und Soziologie,* Groningen: Noordhoff, 1928–1935, I: 132–271.

Stenin, P. von. "Die Kirgisen des Kreises Saissansk im Gebiete von Ssemipalatinsk," *Globus,* LXIX (1896), 227–30.

Steward, Julian H., ed. *Handbook of South American Indians.* Bureau of American Ethnology, Bulletin No. 143, 6 Vols. Washington: Government Printing Office, 1946–1950.

Stinchfield, Sara M. *Speech Disorders.* New York: Harcourt Brace, 1933.

Stout, David B. *San Blas Cuna Acculturation: An Introduction.* Viking Fund Publications in Anthropology, No. 14. New York, 1947.

Swanton, John R. *The Indian Tribes of North America.* Bureau of American Ethnology, Bulletin No. 145. Washington: Government Printing Office, 1952.

Teit, James. *The Salishan Tribes of the Western Plateau.* Forty-Fifth Annual Report of the Bureau of American Ethnology to the Secretary of the Smithsonian Institute. Washington: Government Printing Office, 1930.

Tessman, Günter. *Die Indianer Nordost-Perus.* Hamburg: Friederichsen, 1930.

Thompson, Virginia. *French Indo-China.* New York: Macmillan, 1937.

Thurnwald, Richard. *Economics in Primitive Communities.* New York and London: Oxford University Press, 1932.

Turner, Leonard. *The Social and Psychological Role of the Korean Sorceress.* MS. read at American Anthropological Association meeting, December, 1950; copy of MS. at Department of Anthropology, University of Southern California.

Turney-High, Harry H. *Primitive Warfare: Its Practice and Concepts.* Columbia, S.C.: University of South Carolina Press, 1949.

Tylor, Edward B., "On a Method of Investigating the Development of Institutions Applied to the Laws of Marriage and Descent," *Journal of the Royal Anthropological Institute,* XVIII (1889), 245–72. Reprinted in Moore, *supra,* pp. 1–28.

United Nations. *Demographic Yearbook 1956.* New York: Statistical Office of the United Nations, 1956.

U.S. War Department. *The War of the Rebellion: Official Records of the Union and Confederate Armies.* Washington: 1880–1901, 128 vols.

Vanoverbergh, Morice. *The Isneg Life Cycle.* Publications of the Catholic Anthropological Conference, Vol. III, Nos. 2 and 3. Washington, 1936–1938, pp. 81–186, 187–280.

Van Valkenburgh, Richard. *Navaho Common Law: Notes on Political Organization, Property and Inheritance.* Museum Notes, Museum of Northern Arizona, IX. Flagstaff: Northern Arizona Society of Science and Art, Inc., pp. 17–22.

Veniaminov, Ivan E. P. *Notes on the Islands of the Unalaska District,* Vol. III. St. Petersburg: Russian American Co., 1840a.

———. *Notes on the Athin Aleuts and the Koloshi.* St. Petersburg: Russian American Co., 1840b.

Voegelin, Erminie W. "Suicide in Northeastern California," *American Anthropologist,* XXXIX (1937), 445–56.

Volkart, Edmund H., and S. T. Michael. "Bereavement and Mental Health," in *Explorations in Social Psychiatry,* Alexander H. Leighton, John A. Clausen, and Robert N. Wilson, eds. New York: Basic Books, 1957, pp. 281–307.

Vu Cong Hoe. *Du suicide dans la société annamite.* Hanoï: Imprimerie Tonkinoise, 1937.

Wafer, Lionel. *A New Voyage and Description of the Isthmus of America.* The Hakluyt Society, Ser. 2, No. LXXIII. Oxford, 1934.

Walbank, F. W. *Aratos of Sicyon.* London: Cambridge University Press, 1933.

Wald, Abraham. *Sequential Analysis.* New York: Wiley, 1947.

Ward, Winifred K. *Stammering: A Contribution to the Study of Its Problems and Treatment.* London: Hamilton, 1941.

Whiting, Beatrice. *Paiute Sorcery.* Viking Fund Publications in Anthropology, No. 15. New York, 1950.

Whiting, John W. M. "The Cross-Cultural Method," in *Handbook of Social Psychology,* Vol. I, Gardner Lindzey, ed. Reading, Mass.: Addison-Wesley, 1954, pp. 525–31.

———, and Irvin L. Child. *Child Training and Personality.* New Haven: Yale University Press, 1953.

Wilson, Monica. "Witch Belief and Social Structure," *American Journal of Sociology,* LVI (1951), 307-13.

Wisse, Jakob. *Selbstmord und Todesfurcht bei den Naturvölkern*. Zutphen: W. J. Thieme und Cie, 1933.

Wright, Quincy. *A Study of War*, 2 Vols. Chicago: University of Chicago Press, 1942.

Wyman, Leland C., and Betty Thorne. "Notes on Navaho Suicide," *American Anthropologist*, XLVII (1945), 278–87.

Yule, G. U., and M. G. Kendall. *An Introduction to the Theory of Statistics*, 12th Edition. London: Griffin, 1940.

DATE DUE

GAYLORD